Ramayana Smriti

Amma's Teachings on the Ramayana

Mata Amritanandamayi Center
San Ramon, California, United States

Ramayana Smriti
Teachings of Sri Mata Amritanandamayi
Compiled by Swami Jnanamritananda Puri
Translated by Rajani Menon

Published by
Mata Amritanandamayi Center
P.O. Box 613
San Ramon, CA 94583-0613 USA

International: www.amma.org
In India: www.amritapuri.org

Contents

Introduction

It has long been a custom to observe the month of Karkidaka (July–August), as the month of Rāmāyaṇa. It is also a month when people undergo hardship due to the heavy rains. Many families are forced to wrestle with disease and hunger. Humanity does not have the strength to resist Nature. Awakening our inner strength is the only way to withstand and overcome adversities. No force can destroy us if our inner potential, the strength of our inner self, has awakened. The Rāmāyaṇa is the ideal book, reading which we can realize and awaken our inner strength.

If we consider the challenges faced by the noble characters of the Rāmāyaṇa, our difficulties will seem trivial. Because of this, the Rāmāyaṇa gives us the inner strength to overcome any obstacle. Each character helps us to sharpen the weapons we need for life's battles.

The characters of the Rāmāyaṇa are alive for us and show us what to do and what not to do in life's situations. If we reflect on their words and actions and imbibe them in our life's journey, we will not falter. To gain this capacity, we must approach the Rāmāyaṇa with our hearts.

The Rāmāyaṇa Smṛiti contains a concise collection of Amma's Rāmāyaṇa messages given as part of the Rāmāyaṇa month observances. Amma looks at the Rāmāyaṇa's message against the background of today's times. It will inspire us and give us the strength to move forward on the path of dharma without faltering.

Publisher

Rāma is Rāmāyaṇa

"Is there anyone in this world who is perfect, with all noble qualities?" With this question the Rāmāyaṇa begins. In response, sage Nārada talks about Rāma of Ayōdhyā. The story of Rāma has been able to attract and purify minds through the centuries. No other composition in the world has been passed down through generations and succeeded in purifying minds like the Rāmāyaṇa. If Vālmīki, who wrote the Rāmāyaṇa, lived, then what meaning or logic is there in saying that Rāma never lived and is not a real figure? If Vālmīki lived, then Rāma also did.

Vālmīki clearly describes the qualities of the mahāpuruṣha, the great enlightened personality that he envisages. He should be most accomplished, knowledgeable, constant and firm, compassionate to all beings, courageous, with deep knowledge of all the sciences and authoritative scriptures. He should have conquered his indriyas — his organs of sense and perception. Vālmīki extols many of these qualities. Nārada replies that Rāma is the ideal human being in whom all these qualities come together. A human being will become a mahāpuruṣha if he possesses even one or two of these qualities.

Rāma is known as the idol or epitome of dharma, the ideal and most excellent human. Rāma shows us how to remain faithful to truth and dharma even when he experiences life's trials and endures sorrow. His rule is the intense, focused spiritual practice of an ideal ruler; it is God's worship, the surrender of oneself to one's land. This was Rāma's reign. The synonym for an ideal rule came to be known as *Rāma Rājya.*

The Rāmāyaṇa mirrors our culture — our saṁskāra, refined through thousands of years. If we have dirt on our face, a mirror will reveal it to us, and we will be able to wipe the dirt away. But a mirror cannot show us the impurities of our mind. The Rāmāyaṇa is a mirror that reflects our mind. While an ordinary mirror reflects our face and external appearance, the Rāmāyaṇa shows us our inner reality and our true nature. This mirror exposes our weaknesses and, at the very same time, helps us to overcome them. The Rāmāyaṇa awakens our strength. We can see in the Rāmāyaṇa an all-embracing vision of life's values.

The Rāmāyaṇa portrays the ideal love between parents and their offspring, selfless love between siblings, a married life replete with sacrifice, a perfect guru-disciple relationship, and a sincere attitude to serve. Jñāna, bhakti, karma and yōga — knowledge, devotion, right action, and union with the divine, can be imbibed from the Rāmāyaṇa.

The Rāmāyaṇa is Rāma's 'ayana' — Rāma's journey. Or, to put it another way, it is our journey to Rāma. Rāma is dharma in a human form. His history shows how he sacrificed everything for the sake of dharma. For the sake of dharma, Rāma sacrificed not only his pleasures and happiness but also rejected all worldly bonds. In the Rāmāyaṇa, we hear Rāma say that he will sacrifice everything for truth's sake. Rāma says he will sacrifice even his wife Sītā and brother Lakṣhmaṇa for truth's sake. Rāma knows that dharma will become denuded in this world if he strays even an inch from it. Therefore, Rāma stands firmly fixed in dharma without swerving even an inch.

Many consider Rāma human, not an incarnation because he experiences sorrow and suffering intensely. When God incarnates as a human being, it will be to live like an ordinary human so that others can become close to them and gain inspiration from their lives. God incarnates as a human to show how humans can rise to the state of Godhood. When God incarnates as a human being, he will also manifest the limitations of humankind. In the Rāmāyaṇa, the paramātman – the supreme self, shows the jivātman – the limited individual self, how to rise to perfection.

Why Do We Read the Rāmāyaṇa?

Many ask why we need to read the Rāmāyaṇa. The Rāmāyaṇa is most suited to give the younger generation a good saṁskāra and the right values. There is a real benefit to a disciplined reading of the Rāmāyaṇa. Love for God and devotion will increase. Bitter gourd and gooseberry are naturally bitter. But if we immerse them long enough in a jar filled with sugar or jaggery, they will become sweet. We will not know that they were initially bitter. We will enjoy the taste like a sweet delicacy.

Likewise, if we can bond our mind, which is impure in nature, to God, its impurities will lessen, and finally, the mind will become pure. Unclean water goes through a filtration process, and the water becomes fit to drink. If we drink unclean water, we will fall sick and may even die. If we can bond our impure mind to God, it will be cleansed through love. It will become imbued with joy and peace.

A bath is essential for a clean body. Likewise, satsang[1] and the perusal of satgranthas (books that contain the truth) are essential for a clean mind. Satgranthas belong to three categories. One category reveals dharma and adharma, and fosters awareness and faithfulness to dharma.[2] The second category increases devotion to God and spiritual awareness. The third category describes life experiences in a manner that profoundly touches and influences the heart. Through this, the heart becomes tender and receptive and ideal values and good qualities become firmly established in people's hearts. The Rāmāyaṇa is a composite of all three of these categories in its perfection. We can safely say that no other book has influenced the hearts of people and the saṁskāra or culture of Bhārat (India) as the Rāmāyaṇa has. The adage that the Rāmāyaṇa will last as long as mountains and rivers exist on earth is not astonishing.

---

[1] The company of mahātmās and spiritual discourse.

[2] Dharma is 'that which upholds (creation),' generally referring to the harmony of the universe; a righteous code of conduct; sacred duty; or the eternal law. Adharma is that which deviates from dharma.

The ocean waters evaporate in the sun's heat, ascend to become clouds, and pour down as life-giving rain everywhere. The water collects to become flowing rivers in which people bathe and collect water to drink. Likewise, the Itihāsas and Purāṇas are texts which contain the essence of the Vēdas, and are helpful to ordinary humans. The Vālmīki Rāmāyaṇa can be compared to a great river. When canals are dug on the sides of a river and its water gets diverted to fields, it benefits humanity even more. Ezhuthachan's Adhyātma Rāmāyaṇa Kiḷippaṭṭu[3] can be compared to this. It has added the honey of devotion to the milk of Rāmāyaṇa. In the month of Karkidaka, our land becomes pure with the rendering of the Rāmāyaṇa. Malayālis usually read Ezhuthachan's Adhyātma Rāmāyaṇa Kiḷippaṭṭu.

The Rāmāyaṇa is peerless poetry and one of the world's most beautiful compositions. It lays

---

[3] *Adhyātma Rāmāyaṇa Kiḷippaṭṭu* is a devotional composition in Malayāḷam poetry by the great 16th century poet Thunchaththu Ezhuthachan. It is based on the *Adhyātma Rāmāyaṇa*, which is a Sanskrit text usually attributed to sage Vyāsa presenting a spiritual rendering of the traditional *Vālmīki Rāmāyaṇa*.

open for us hundreds of colorful word pictures of ancient Bhāratīya saṁskāra. It exhorts us to leave the narrow path of a self-centered life and travel on the path of selflessness. Many characters in the Rāmāyaṇa shine with the radiance of noble human values. Their sacrifice and fidelity to dharma melt our hearts. Anyone who reads the Rāmāyaṇa with faith and attention to detail will become humbler and more aware of dharmic values.

When sacred texts like the Rāmāyaṇa are read aloud daily, it will benefit all the family members who hear it. The atmosphere inside the home will lighten up. When a fragrant incense is lit, its fragrance does not remain confined to a single room. It spreads to every other room and the surroundings. Likewise, the verses of the Rāmāyaṇa infuse the atmosphere with positivity. If those who read the Rāmāyaṇa also absorb its principles and live accordingly, their life will be an exemplar for others. It will inspire others. They will also try to live and perform actions in the same manner. Many will turn to goodness and adopt dharma.

If we closely observe, we will realize that many of the characters in the Rāmāyaṇa surpass each other in virtues. Daśharatha's[4] sons achieved victory because they traveled the path of humility, love and dharma. Their kingdom grew in dharma, and adharma waned in power. Life will not only have victories, but it will also contain suffering. The Rāmāyaṇa shows us how to accept both when they arrive. If we are able to hold tightly onto dharma amidst all danger, we can continue to be the king without the need to bow our heads down to anyone. The Rāmāyaṇa shows us that even if we have to leave as a beggar, we can return as a king. Yet, many strive today for temporary success, even by abandoning dharma. They do not have the patience to wait for even a short while.

Today, society chases instant, fleeting pleasures, and enters the world of intoxicants and drugs. We should fear such psychoactive substances even more than war, because children can become enslaved to drugs. Reading and studying books like the Rāmāyaṇa is the solution. Through this, children will be able to imbibe noble qualities. They will gain self-confidence. They will not fall to temptation but will

[4] King of Ayōdhyā and the father of Lord Rāma.

gain the strength, clarity, purity, and awareness of dharma to face and overcome challenges.

A Guide for Life

The Rāmāyaṇa is not a book to be read once and then put aside. Today, many people read out the Bhāgavatam to Bhagavān, the Lord. They read the Rāmāyaṇa for Bhagavān. They believe that if they do so, they will gain puṇya (merit). Books like the Rāmāyaṇa and the Mahābhārata should be read for our own sake. The sun does not need a candle to light its way. God gives all abundance to this universe. A golden pot doesn't need any further embellishment. We do not need to offer water to a river to slake its thirst. On the contrary, we can drink to our fill from the river and slake *our* thirst. We can use the river water to clean the dirty drains around it. Likewise, we should imbibe life lessons from the Rāmāyaṇa.

If we write honey on a piece of paper and lick it, we will not experience the sweetness of honey. We may hear it from a recorder or read it from a book, but the Rāmāyaṇa comes alive only when we live according to its values. It is as different as saying, "a flower," and seeing a flower. When we say, "a flower," it does not become our experience. Likewise, the lines of the Rāmāyaṇa come alive only when we live with fidelity to the principles it expounds. It uplifts our life, and we become a good example for others. When we read the Rāmāyaṇa, we should strive to live faithful to its principles. Instead, we are caught up in external rituals and unthinkingly follow them. They become mechanical. Those rituals do not touch our hearts or transform us.

It is rare to find people who live the principles of the Rāmāyaṇa. The cow drawn on a piece of paper will not eat grass; neither will it give milk. Likewise, buying books like the Rāmāyaṇa and storing them in our homes will not serve any purpose. We will benefit more from reading the Rāmāyaṇa if we imbibe its principles and try to practice them in our lives.

There is an incomparable, amazing strength to the life of a mahāpuruṣha whose actions spring from truth, dharma, and love. Dharma will be intensely nourished in society. People will have an intense yearning to know the truth. Many will be attracted to the avatārapuruṣha — the incarnation of God. Love for God will enliven the light of consciousness in society; people will live with awareness. Rāma was such a mahāpuruṣha, and the Rāmāyaṇa is his story. It is no wonder the Rāmāyaṇa has enriched our saṁskāra, and refined and uplifted our society for thousands of years.

Dharma is facing grave challenges in this age. Therefore, it is essential to read the Rāmāyaṇa. If children need to grow up with the right values to lead a family life with mutual trust, cooperation, awareness of dharma, and love for God, their homes should have such an atmosphere. Grown-ups should live as good examples for their children.

Life will respond to us according to how we view and evaluate life experiences and perform our actions. The subtle laws of the universe transcend the knowledge we gain through life experiences. Dharma is founded on those laws. We need to give the laws of this universe the same, if not more importance than we give to the laws of the country. We praise the creations of humanity sky-high. We praise the sculptor when we see the statue of an elephant. When we see a lovely painting of a tree near a placid lake, we praise the artist. We will also give them many prizes.

Yet, we will forget the creator of the elephant and the tree. When we praise the capabilities of humanity, we should always remember śhakti, the primal force, the energy which acts as the substratum of our intelligence. This primal force will record each of our actions like a tape recorder records our conversations. We are experiencing the result of our own actions. It's important to remember this when we hear the life experiences of many people. The Rāmāyaṇa is a guiding light for us as it teaches us to journey on the path of dharma without breaking the universal laws.

In earlier days, grandmothers would read out the Rāmāyaṇa, Mahābhārata, and Bhāgavatam to the children in their family. They would also explain the lessons to be learnt from those stories. The younger generation imbibed moral values from such stories and other sārōpadēśhas — texts that encapsulate the core teachings of Sanātana Dharma and offer moral guidance. These teachings greatly influenced their future lives and character formation. We are losing this family ambience and culture. This age belongs to the mobile phone and internet. We have forgotten dharmic stories and the Purāṇas. Its detrimental effect is evident in our society.

A Book on Dharma

Bhārat is the land of dharma. Bhārat is the land that gifted the Vēdas, the six great philosophical systems known as the Ṣhaḍ Darśhanas (which include Vēdānta), the eighteen Purāṇas and Upapurāṇas, the Rāmāyaṇa, the Mahābhārata (also known as the fifth Vēda), and the Bhagavad Gītā to the world. These great books are oceans of knowledge that the ṛiṣhis, the sages who are the mantradṛiṣhṭas (to whom the mantras were revealed), bequeathed to the world. These books pulsate with the purity, inner strength, sacrifice, equal vision, and intense tapas (austerity) of the ṛiṣhis.

Bhārat's real wealth are the great seers whose only aim was the welfare of the world and the sanātana, the eternal and ever-new, spirituality they revealed.

The Rāmāyaṇa is an Itihāsa that has vanquished the passage of time. An Itihāsa records the life of mahāpuruṣhas who lived in this world, and aims to spread dharmic values in society.

More than the history of mahātmās (great souls), Itihāsas are texts based on their lives, filled with stories that touch the heart of dharma, artha, kāma, and mōkṣha, advising us on how to attain these four puruṣhārthas, the fourfold aims of human life.

Our minds become tender and receptive when we listen to and read them. Our values grow; the mind becomes pure. In the Rāmāyaṇa we can see all these qualities in their perfection. This is why the āchāryas, the teachers, accepted Rāmāyaṇa as the ideal means to spread awareness of dharma and devotion towards God.

All that we need in a human life is contained in the puruṣhārthas. Wealth, name and fame, and aiśhvarya – auspicious prosperity and worldly progress, are a part of artha. All sensory and mental pleasures and the striving to achieve them are kāma. Mōkṣha is the perfection of life.

The Rāmāyaṇa is akin to a supermarket. You will find within its pages all that is needed for a human being to live in this world with joy and peace and reach life's ultimate goal — self-realization. We can learn from the Rāmāyaṇa what devotion is; about action; union with God or oneness with God; destiny; duties and responsibilities; family relationships; ruling a kingdom; leadership qualities; all you need to know and understand. The Rāmāyaṇa teaches us that even though happiness and prosperity are important in life, even more important is dharma, and the true goal of a human life is to realize God.

Dharma is the world's foundation. Dharma gives goodness and prosperity to all beings. An ideal saṁskāra, an inner refinement, can be cemented only through dharma. Those who practice dharma will assuredly gain a life of peace, contentment, fame and success. On the contrary, those who abandon dharma will finally experience sorrow and strife. We reach perfection by staying true to dharma. The principle of dharma is very subtle. It is challenging to understand. Mahāpuruṣhas, who are great personalities with immense inner strength, the strength of the ātman (the true self), are needed to teach the world the dharma appropriate for the time and age. They inspire and motivate the world. Dharma is reestablished through the example of their life. A rich and noble saṁskāra is formed. Their life story becomes an Itihāsa.

We have gained two such Itihāsas: the Mahābhārata and the Rāmāyaṇa. They are two books of great profundity. They are beacons on the path of truth and dharma. It will be challenging to answer the question, "Which of the two is preeminent?" In volume and grandeur, the Mahābhārata is at the forefront. Yet, the Rāmāyaṇa has won over millions of lives and hearts. The glorious history of Prince Rāma has traveled across the oceans and has been admired and adopted in many lands. The Rāmāyaṇa is ideal for teaching dharmic values to children and society.

At a time when there was no press or media, the Rāmāyaṇa was passed down through the generations and carried from land to land. It became entrenched in different cultures as a part of their life and saṁskāra. We can see the significant influence of the Rāmāyaṇa on wall art, paintings and ancient art repositories.

Many countries and their citizens have their own versions of the Rāmāyaṇa in their own language and a culture based on it. The Rāmāyaṇa is the national book of Indonesia, a Muslim country, and of Thailand, a Buddhist nation. However, the source is the Vālmīki Rāmāyaṇa. The Rāmāyaṇa is the eternal flame that illumines our ancient, glorious saṁskāra and Sanātana Dharma — the ancient wisdom of Bhārat. It still exerts a profound and purifying influence on the mind of humanity, proving the truth of the prophecy that the Rāmāyaṇa will increase its reach and influence and uplift the human mind as long as mountains and rivers exist on earth. Mountains and rivers not only bestow beauty upon the earth, they benefit all living beings. The Rāmāyaṇa is similar. Rāma's unequaled history will please the mind and awaken the right values in our hearts. It imbues the heart with devotion.

Dharma waxes and wanes like the moon up in the sky. Dharma is enriched at times and denuded at other times. Adharma — evil — becomes rampant, and people suffer inordinately. We believe the compassionate Lord sees our suffering and incarnates to resurrect waning dharma. The birth of a mahāpuruṣha is like cooling, life-giving rain in an arid and burning summer. It is like the sudden offset of the spring season in a desert. Evil loses its grip on society and goodness blossoms.

When dharmic principles remain on paper, they don't significantly transform people. But when a mahātmā demonstrates those principles in their life, it revitalizes and transforms an entire society. Their history is handed down through generations and uplifts humankind, enriching their saṁskāra — refining their intellects, minds and hearts. Rāma's history is such a one. Many shining exemplars in the Rāmāyaṇa can be taken as our ideals. Similarly, there are also depraved characters that teach us not to be like them. We need to recognize right from wrong. The Rāmāyaṇa helps the individual, family, and society lead lives of disciplined self-control.

The Rāmāyaṇa is a magnificent composition that helps cement the right values and noble qualities in the young. An unwavering practice of dharma, devotion, renunciation, and detachment are all qualities they will imbibe. Even if we momentarily keep aside the spiritual and devotional aspects of the Rāmāyaṇa, the strength and depth of family bonding revealed in the book make it invaluable. Devotion to mother and father, love between brothers, and a model relationship between husband and wife are all shown in the Rāmāyaṇa. With the passage of time, family bonds have become brittle. When parents become old and frail, they are felt as an unnecessary burden. The Rāmāyaṇa enters family lives with the message of love and sacrifice. The Rāmāyaṇa showcases individuals who live true to right values and to society, and embodies a saṁskāra embedded in noble values. It is a saṁskāra that places great importance on values and ideals over and above worldly gain.

Let Life Flow Peacefully

Through Śhrī Rāma, the Rāmāyaṇa teaches us the principle that we are God or brahman — the absolute truth. God permeates all we see, which the Rāmāyaṇa demonstrates through its storyline. Rāma was the eldest son of Daśharatha. He was going to be the next king and it was the time for his coronation. Yet, whether we are kings or ordinary human beings, life will bring unexpected experiences and circumstances before us. They may destroy all hope. They may give joy but can also turn into sorrow within minutes. Ayōdhyā was brimming over with joyous expectations and celebrations of the impending coronation.

But within seconds, the darkness of unbearable sorrow spread over the land. Rāma was destined to spend fourteen years in exile in the forest. When the coronation was blocked, Daśharatha collapsed in despair. Kausalyā also went through deep anguish. Lakṣhmaṇa was furious. Bharata was in the throes of anger resulting from his strong opposition to adharma. Only Rāma stood calm like a serene ocean. He transmitted inner strength to all of them.

When everyone was distraught and unsettled, Rāma brought back harmony. His behavior resembled the one who remained alert to wake up the sleeping ones.

If a hill blocks a flowing river, the river will go around the hill, babbling in joy as it flows onward. Likewise, Rāma welcomed his years in exile, which appeared to be an obstacle in the flow of his life. He did not succumb to the circumstances but embraced them. He flowed onward without deviating even slightly from dharma.

If we seriously read the Mahābhārata and the Rāmāyaṇa, we will realize they include everything. Afterwards, we must learn the Bhagavad Gītā thoroughly. If we can imbibe the Gītā, we will see our life being transformed. It will be like swimming in a calm and placid ocean with no waves or turbulent currents. Our minds will go into a state of quietude, peace, and beauty. If we really want to, we can bring about a permanent change in our lives. Our life passes through many unexpected changes. Don't we inevitably accept them all?

Once, one of Amma's sons came to her and said, "Amma, I loved a girl for many years. I went to the extent of saying that if I couldn't marry her, I would kill myself. So, even though my parents disagreed, I married her. But after only two years of marriage, I could no longer live with her. I did not want her anymore." He had once loved her more than his own life; now, he resented her with all his life. After two years, he got a divorce from her. So, even though he once said he couldn't live without her, he is now living without her. Our mind is the cause of both our bondage and our liberation. It is the cause of both dharma and adharma. If we wish to do so, we can bring about change. The principle of dharma is very subtle. Even the wise ones are unable to discriminate between dharma and adharma in times of crisis. In such situations, the Rāmāyaṇa illuminates the path for us.

Even though there are many characters in the Rāmāyaṇa, the central figure is Rāma. He is as patient as the earth, as detached as the sky, as auspicious as the full moon. He displays patience where patience is needed, courage where courage is needed, diplomacy where it is needed, forbearance and stoic endurance where it is needed. He also showed friendship where it was needed.

Kaikēyī's words were adharmic; Rāma was the rightful king. Therefore, Rāma could have easily brushed aside Kaikēyī's words. Why did he not do so? Because it is the dharma of a son to fulfill the promises given by his father. Daśharatha may have thought, "I gave the right to Kaikēyī to ask for two boons many years ago. I never thought that she would use them at this fateful moment. Oh, Rāma! Do not think about your father; do not give up the throne." But Rāma's thoughts went like this, "My father granted two boons to Kaikēyī because he appreciated her unselfish acts. Now, because of his grief and attachment to me, the king is telling me not to fulfill his pledge. Therefore, what he says now is not the right course of action. I should make true the promises he made then." This shows that Rāma valued dharma more than anything else.

Lessons in Goodness

Ayōdhyā and Laṅka reveal two saṁskāras, or cultures, to us. Ayōdhyā's culture is established in dharma and sacrifice for the sake of another. Laṅka showcases the culture of luxury and excesses, and the arrogance of authoritarian power. In Laṅka, we see the saṁskāra in which the ego predominates, the sense of "I am capable of doing everything by myself." In Ayōdhyā, we see individuals sacrificing their interests for the sake of truth and dharma.

Rāvaṇa and his followers reveled in their might and, in their egoistic arrogance, did many cruel and adharmic deeds. On the contrary, Rāma's ancestral lineage was like a fertile land from which ideal qualities could be harvested. Lakṣhmaṇa is the prime example of brotherly love and devotion towards his elder brother. Bharata is the symbol of selfless service and sacrifice. Sītā epitomizes unswerving loyalty to her husband, patience, endurance, and determination. Daśharatha was unwilling to forsake the truth even when in the throes of anguish.

Kaikēyī saved Daśharatha's life on the battlefield. This dedication on Kaikēyī's part prompted Daśharatha to give her two boons. Kaikēyī had risked her own life to save his. Such total dedication made Daśharatha forget himself enough to grant her two boons. It was not her physical beauty, nor her show of external love that motivated Daśharatha. Even though he was attracted to Kaikēyī, his love for Rāma was more intense and stronger. The pain of parting from Rāma caused his death.

At the same time, Rāma became willing to forfeit the throne to uphold his father's word. He did so with complete detachment and total ease. As the eldest son, he was the rightful heir to the throne. He had the strength to overcome any opposition to reclaim his right. But Rāma chose the path of humility, of sacrifice. Daśharatha was keen to crown Rāma king; it was his ardent desire. Sending his son to the forest was more than he could bear. But he had to fulfill a promise given long ago. Rāma understood his father's helplessness. This is why Rāma's words to Kaikēyī, "Even if my father does not say so, to fulfill his promise to you, I will obey your words." Rāma says he would happily forgo the kingdom that rightfully belonged to him and his very life for his father's sake. Later, Bharata pleads with Rāma, "Come back, sit on the throne, I do not need the kingdom." But Rāma remains determined to uphold his father's word without being even slightly influenced by his brother's impassioned pleas.

When Rāma prepared to leave for the forest, Sītā could have said, "There is no need for you to leave for the forest. Stay back, as this kingdom is rightfully yours. Why should you go? Don't let go of the kingdom." This is probably what most women would say nowadays. But Sītā did not make any such demands. Sītā's attitude was this — heaven is where Rāma is. Sītā silently accompanied her husband.

What does Bharata teach us? He did not think, "My brother has left the place, so now I can rule the kingdom." He sought out Rāma, brought back his pādukās, and kept them on the throne. Like a servant, like a disciple, he considered his elder brother his God and guru, and ruled the kingdom, surrendering himself to Rāma. Bharata lived an ascetic life of great sacrifice. Lakṣhmaṇa dedicated himself to serving his brother who had lost the kingdom. For fourteen years, he performed severe austerities, often foregoing even sleep. In this manner, we cannot say who among them is the nobler one, such is the glory of their characters.

We see here an ideal, highly principled relationship between father and son, mother and son, between brothers, between husbands and wives. They are a model and inspiration for each family. They have taught us through their lives. They are still inspiring and motivating others. Even now, joint families exist in many places. If the father dies, the eldest son takes on the father's responsibilities and sustains the family, forgiving the transgressions of the younger members.

Many children come to Amma and say, "Amma, ours is a joint family. My father is giving away everything for the welfare of his siblings. If this continues, there will be nothing left for us." At the same time, the younger brother's wife says, "My husband will only obey his elder brother's words. They are my husband's sacred law. More than us, his affection is towards his elder brother. Whatever his elder brother says is right; he does not listen to our words. Amma, in this day and age, is this how it should be?"

Even if he keeps nothing for himself, the elder brother will meet the needs of his brother's children. Even if the younger brother does something wrong, the elder will go and tell their mother, "Mother, after my father's death, my younger brother has become akin to my son. I shall take care of his children." Whatever their wives' opinions, the younger brothers give great value to the words of their elder brother. They know well that he lives solely for them. They will not say anything contrary to their brother's words. The Rāmāyaṇa comes to mind when Amma hears of such strong family bonds and the lives of those families.

There are still some families that live in obedience to the ancient ways and values. In some North Indian families, we can see them observing the principles of the Rāmāyaṇa in their family life. More than sixty per cent of the households of joint families lead lives similar to those of the characters in the Rāmāyaṇa. It is incredible that such relationships still exist in a day and age where values are fast eroding. They can live in such unity and prosperity because they have grasped the core principles of the Rāmāyaṇa.

But I have also seen some instances where the elder brother is forsaken by his younger siblings and their families. The elder brother would be a pleasant and gentle person who lives for his brothers' families. He will not save anything for himself. Finally, the others will secure all the wealth and family property for themselves and reject him. In some cases, the elder sister will take up a job, educate the younger ones, and see that they reach high places. Due to family responsibilities, she will even forget to marry. Finally, when she becomes old, there is no one to take care of her. She will have to live the life of an abandoned destitute.

In some families, the eldest member will go abroad to work and send their monthly salary back home. Things at home will go smoothly. The house will be rebuilt, the brothers and sisters will be well-educated, and their weddings will be conducted grandly. Yet, when his job ends, and he finally returns to his own country, the eldest brother may not even have a home of his own. The rebuilt house that he paid for would now be in the name of a brother or sister. It is futile to say that it was his hard-earned money that was spent to make the run-down house new and habitable, and that he also had a right to live there.

Living in tune with the principles espoused in the Rāmāyaṇa is good. But because there are selfish people in this day and age, we should also be practical. We should foresee that we may be treated unjustly if the people around us are selfish. We should change according to the times and always hold onto practical intelligence. We can see such practical brilliance in Rāma's life.

A teacher brought four glasses to class to conduct an experiment and poured water into them. He put stones in one glass, mud in another, cotton in the third, and rock sugar in the fourth glass. Then, he showed the four glasses to the children and explained, "See the glass of water filled with rocks. Nothing good happens either to the stones or to the water. The stone remains as such. Likewise, many humans live without being of any benefit either to themselves or to others." He picked up the second glass and said, "Look how the good water becomes muddy when mixed with mud.

Likewise, some people muddy the world's waters, destroying society. They will destroy themselves and others." He picked up the third glass and said, "I put cotton into the water of the third glass. The cotton absorbed all the water in the glass in a second. Likewise, there are people in this world who live by cheating others. For them, nothing matters except their own gain." Then he picked up the fourth glass and said, "I added rock sugar into the water in this glass. He gave each student some water to drink and asked, "How is it?" "It is so sweet," said the children. The teacher reminded them, "There are still people in this world who offer themselves for the welfare of the world."

What is important is the role we choose among the four. We should be able to bring sweetness into the lives of others. We should be able to bring joy to the world even if we ourselves cease to be. For this, we need to become like rock sugar. The Rāmāyaṇa shows us the way. Rāma and all his brothers desired only the happiness of others. But nowadays, we mostly see people who resemble cotton. Their aim is their own happiness, even at the cost of others. Thus, there will always be many kinds of people around us. In each situation, use your discernment. As long as the people with you do not understand the good you are doing for them or the trouble you are taking on their behalf, you should go forward with caution. Goodness should not become a gullible weakness to be exploited; you should also be practical.

Pointing out adharma – unrighteousness, is also dharma. Do not say 'yes' to everything. It is not right or ethical to keep quiet even if you see adharma, just because you are unsure of others' opinions. It is wrong if someone rapes a child. You should have the courage to say that it is wicked and unrighteous. It is our dharma to bring attention to and respond against unrighteous acts. It is our duty. We need a thorn to take out another thorn. There are rules to be obeyed on the road. It is dharma to impose a fine on those who break those rules. If cars are being driven over the speed limit, imposing a fine on such drivers is to make life safe for others. They will reduce their speed because they wouldn't want to lose the amount of the fine. Otherwise, they might crash into another vehicle and injure its occupants. They may also bring danger upon themselves. Some people do not consider others or bother about dharma and live only for selfish pleasure. They are like Rāvaṇa. We need such punishments to bring awareness to such people.

The Rāmāyaṇa shows us an exalted vision of family. It is a model that every family should imbibe. We should impart it to our children. But none of us do so. What do we see in many families now? "Children, always speak the truth, never lie." But often, the adults are not true to their words. Once, a phone rang in a house, and the young boy living there answered the phone. He went to his father and said, "Dad, someone on the phone is asking for you. He wanted me to give you the phone if you are here." The father replied, "Son, tell him I am not here." The father had taught his son not to tell a lie. But his actions belie his words and prompt the child also to lie. These are the behavior models that we see now. We see the paucity of good models in our society.

Our culture has become one that creates Kaṁsas[5]. This is what we see in many places today. It should change, and we should create an atmosphere and circumstances that create mahātmās like Rāma. Then, we will see a transformation, even though slight, in society.

---

[5] Kaṁsa was the wicked uncle of Śhrī Kṛiṣhṇa who was so hellbent on avoiding the prophecy of his impending death at the hands of his nephew that he had ordered all newborns to be killed in his kingdom in an attempt to prevent the birth of Śhrī Kṛiṣhṇa.

For that, the saṁskāra of Rāma should permeate family life.

The Rāmāyaṇa has many levels of meaning. On one level, Śhrī Rāma is the paramātmā – the supreme self. The goal of the Rāmāyaṇa is to awaken love for God in people. On another level, Rāma is dharma that has taken a human form. The goal of Rāma is to reinstate dharma in society.

On another level, spirituality is the message of the Rāmāyaṇa. It gives us the message of the union of the jivātmā – the embodied self, with the paramātmā – the supreme self, through conquering our weaknesses, latent tendencies, and desires. However you may consider it, the Rāmāyaṇa benefits and awakens goodness in society. Each viewpoint has its strength. And even though the Rāmāyaṇa is all this, it also transcends these levels.

Family Relationships

Each character in the Rāmāyaṇa teaches us noble values. Rāma's greatness of heart is revealed in the compassion that he shows Vibhīṣhaṇa, who has taken refuge in him; in the mercy he shows Rāvaṇa, who was beaten and exhausted on the battlefield; the detachment with which he refuses to take anything from Laṅka; his decision to accept the kingdom only if Bharata is ready and willingly parts with it; his ability to sacrifice. The Rāmāyaṇa teaches us what is essential and what is unimportant in life.

The events described in the Rāmāyaṇa happened many thousands of years ago. It may not be possible for us to emulate everything. Yet, there are many valuable lessons to learn from it. Suppose our father has taken some money on loan, giving his word that he would repay it. After some time, the father refuses to pay back the loan. The one who loaned the money kept on asking him to repay it. The son was extraordinarily truthful and assured the man, "If my father refuses to give the money back, I will repay you." He paid back the loan. So, even if the father would not repay the money, his honest son repaid the loan. This was Rāma's intention, and this is how he acted. Those who consider Rāma to be their ideal can never think otherwise.

The intelligent business people of today will consider Rāma's actions foolish. They will call him a silly fool. Today, many may think, "His father did not ask him to go to the forest; neither did his mother. Why should I listen to my father's younger wife, my younger mother? Because of two boons that my father had promised her long ago, why should I fulfill her desires? My father wants me to be crowned king; hence, I will become the king and not give up my rights to the throne." But Rāma gave utmost value to dharma and not to wealth, power, or the kingdom. Wealth and power do not last forever; they come and go. We should hold fast to dharma. Only a life firmly rooted in dharma can transcend time and space. This is why we still remember and revere Rāma. This is why we want to follow in his footsteps.

Lakṣhmaṇa could not stand and watch silently as his elder brother decided to go alone to the forest. The forest was full of wild animals that may harm his brother. Who would help his brother if some harm came to him? He had no second thoughts as he followed Rāma into the forest.

What did Sītā, his wife, think? Let my husband go; no one said I should go with him. The forest paths are strewn with rocks and thorns, and there will only be roots and fruits to eat. I do not want to endure such hardship. Let me continue to live on in the palace. Sītā did not think so. She did not want to accept any of the comforts and luxuries denied to her husband. Sītā believed that a wife should share her husband's joy and sorrow. Even though many tried to dissuade her, Sītā could not be persuaded to stay back. She followed Rāma like his shadow.

As for Bharata, he decided he would never accept the kingdom that was Rāma's by birthright. Kaikēyī's efforts were futile, so strong was the bond between the two brothers. Bharata reached the forest to seek out Rāma and bring him back to Ayōdhyā and the throne. But despite his fervent pleas, Rāma did not return but gave his brother the authority to rule on his behalf. Bharata was not besotted with the power and position granted to him. Finally, he placed his brother's pādukās on his head, placed them on the throne, and ruled as Rāma's representative. When we read the Rāmāyaṇa, our homes were imbued with such selfless brotherly love. Since we lost this tradition, the situation has become so bad that in some families, brothers do not hesitate to raise butcher's knives against each other.

Attachment Is the Path to Sorrow

In the Rāmāyaṇa, the story takes a tragic turn when Kaikēyī blocks Śhrī Rāma's coronation. This incident serves to open our eyes to many of life's realities.

It is said that when Daśharatha was on the battlefield, Kaikēyī, who loved her husband as dearly as her own life, saved his life twice. A grateful Daśharatha promised her two boons. Kaikēyī replied that she would ask for them later. Eventually, she asked her husband to fulfill his promise on the eve of Śhrī Rāma's coronation. The two boons she demanded were to crown Bharata, her own son, as king instead of Rāma, and the other to exile Rāma to the forest for fourteen years. Daśharatha had not even dreamt that Kaikēyī would seek such boons from him. He collapsed upon hearing her words. His sorry state and deep grief did not sway Kaikēyī. She stayed firm, unflinching in her demands.

Rāma was dearest to Daśharatha. At the same time, his desire for Kaikēyī was also very intense. This was why Daśharatha had to endure such grief. He lost all composure and became desperate when he heard that Kaikēyī was angry with him. He forgot his role and power as a king; his only thought was to please Kaikēyī. Daśharatha had already promised Kaikēyī that he would grant any desire of hers. But he collapsed when he heard the two boons that Kaikēyī demanded of him. She demanded the crown for Bharata and a fourteen-year forest exile for Rāma. Thus, Daśharatha's excessive attachment to Kaikēyī became the cause of unbearable sorrow, while Kaikēyī remained indifferent to his laments.

What should we learn from this? It is said that Daśharatha was as dear to Kaikēyī as her own life. Yet she demanded from him the very two boons that were unbearable to him. So, where did her love go? This goes to show that worldly love is never unselfish. There is selfishness behind such love. This is the nature of all worldly love. If a threat is felt to one's own comfort and position, then all love vanishes. Kaikēyī loved her husband. She loved Rāma like her own son. Yet, when she realized that once Rāma became king, Kausalyā would become the queen mother, fear awoke in her that she and her son Bharata would lose the privileges they enjoyed. She had no compunction in throwing away all dictates of dharma. She remained indifferent to the unbearable sorrow experienced by her husband. She brutally brushed away Daśharatha's pleas even as he fell at her feet.

Daśharatha was at fault for not informing Kaikēyī immediately of his decision to crown Rāma. Kaikēyī hears the news only after his subjects come to know of it. How could Kaikēyī, who prided herself on being his favorite queen, bear this? Also, Daśharatha was unable to understand or gauge the character of his son Bharata. He wanted to crown Rāma before Bharata returned. But, had Bharata been in the palace, Rāma's coronation would have gone smoothly. Bharata was steady in his devotion to Rāma and faithful to his ideals.

Daśharatha is drained of all strength when he hears that Kaikēyī is displeased. His intellect froze. Rāma's coronation had been decided unanimously by an assembly of great scholars and ministers. The decision had been announced to the populace, and arrangements were in full swing. The king did not have the authority to reject the assembly's decision. So, from this perspective, Kaikēyī was too late in asking for her boons and Daśharatha could have told Kaikēyī that her demands were adharmic; but a benumbed Daśharatha could say nothing.

He was in agony, torn between his love for Kaikēyī and Rāma. He was at a crossroads, exhausted in body and mind, not knowing what to do and which way to proceed. His heart was beating in despair like a fish on the shore desperately struggling to reach the water. But even then, love for Rāma was uppermost in his mind. He was fortunate to leave his body with thoughts of Rāma engulfing his mind. In this manner, he was able to merge with Rāma. His prāṇa left him as he chanted Rāma...Rāma... Rāma... His attachment to everything except Rāma was broken asunder. His mind was full of love; only Rāma resided there. Like a horse wearing blinkers, seeing nothing else, with only Rāma filling his heart, lamenting in sorrow over his son, he was able to merge with Rāma. An unforeseen circumstance turned Daśharatha's mind away from worldly goals and fixed it firmly on Rāma. What should we understand from this? If the problems we face become reasons for us to turn our minds towards God, then those problems are blessings in reality.

When Rāma's coronation was blocked, Ayōdhyā's atmosphere became unsettled and distraught. People's minds also became disturbed and unbalanced. Kausalyā and Sumitrā[6] collapsed under the burden of their grief. Lakṣhmaṇa blazed up in fury. The ministers and citizens became sad. When every heart was undergoing the throes of different passions, Rāma remained like a calm ocean, witnessing everything. His face wore no display of emotion. He tried calmly, with humility and just words, to reclaim peace and harmony.

By the time Bharata returned to the palace in Ayōdhyā, Rāma had left for the forest. Bharata was furious at his mother's betrayal of dharma and went to Rāma in the forest. But Rāma consoled him and did not accept rulership over the kingdom even though Bharata pleaded with him. Our eyes will become moist and our hearts tender on seeing the three brothers' mutual

---

6 King Daśharatha had three wives: Kaikēyī is the mother of Bharata; Kausalyā the mother of Rāma; and Sumitrā the mother of the twins Lakṣhmaṇa and Śhatrughna.

love, wisdom, and sacrifice. Rāma gave only one stern command to Bharata, "Do not upset Mother Kaikēyī in any way. She is your mother, so give her the utmost respect." This reveals Rāma's broad vision. He was always willing to forgive ignorance and ego.

Daśharatha's life became overwhelmed by sorrow because of his attachment to Kaikēyī. Love with attachment will only lead us to sorrow. In reality, external love is always for an object or person. It is not selfless. We love the cow for the milk. Who will feed a cow that doesn't give milk? Cows that do not give milk are sold to the butcher. There is selfishness behind all worldly love. If it is obstructed, it doesn't take long for love to become hatred. Then the one who said, "There is no life without you," will say, "I can live only if you die."

Good Lessons

The Rāmāyaṇa contains many noble characters that can inspire us and that we can aspire to be. There are also cruel and evil characters that teach us never to be like them. When she heard that Rāma would be crowned king, Kaikēyī was extremely happy. When her maid Mantharā informed her that Rāma would be crowned, she took off the jeweled necklace that adorned her neck and offered it to Mantharā as a token of her delight. Mantharā asked, "My queen, what is there to be so happy about? It is not your son who is going to be the king; it is the son of Kausalyā. If Rāma becomes king, Kausalyā becomes the queen-mother. You will be her slave." After listening to these lies for some time, Kaikēyī's mind became corrupted.

A crack formed in her love for Rāma, whom she had so far considered as her own son. Mantharā's malicious words had their desired effect. It did not take long for Kaikēyī to demand that Daśharatha crown her own son Bharata king and exile Rāma to the forest. Once, Kaikēyī had been Daśharatha's dharmapatnī — his consort in dharma, ready to sacrifice her own life to save the life of her husband. But now, she did not flinch even after she saw Daśharatha falling senseless upon hearing her demands. She was not concerned about whatever happened to anyone. She wanted the kingdom for her son.

She abandoned her dharma towards her husband. She abandoned all dharma. What was the result of her actions? Bharata refused to be the king. Kaikēyī had to bear the harsh words of her son and others. She lived in a hell of her own creation, full of remorse for her wrong actions. We need only look at Kaikēyī's life to understand what will happen if we listen to malicious words without considering the well-being of others and think of only our happiness and comfort. Finally, even her own son detested Kaikēyī.

Amma knows thousands of incidents where husbands disowned and abandoned their innocent wives. The women were innocent. They did not comply with the selfish desires of some other men. Once rejected, these men sent letters full of lies to the women's husbands who work in foreign lands. They fabricated lies, and finally, the husbands started suspecting their wives. Almost all of them ended in divorce. The women are left with one or two children to care for and no one to support them. They are abandoned. There are thousands of such lives. Our hearts will break when we listen to their stories. Therefore, we must be cautious of each word that we speak. We must reflect on whether what we say is a lie because a tiny speck of doubt is enough to create a rift in the hearts of the people we love. No one can predict how big and deep this chasm will become.

There will always be people who try to exploit happy families. We should not stop to hear their fabrications. We should have our own perspective. We should not allow anyone to dismantle it. Friends may coerce a boy who believes that watching movies is against his convictions. "Hey, come on, let's go watch this movie. It has such good reviews." When he hears his friend's description of the movie, a small picture of the film will form in his mind. Hearing his friend's constant refrain, the movie will be created in his mind, and the desire will arise to see it. Finally, he will go to the cinema and watch the movie. This does not mean watching movies is terrible; many good messages are conveyed through them. But if we do not desire to watch one, why must we hear its description? If someone starts talking to you about a movie, you can always say that you are not interested in this topic. If they continue in the same vein, it is better to move away. The mind is strong, but even then, we do not need to stay and gauge its strength.

A spiritual seeker should avoid bad company because it is not very easy to bring the mind under our control. If our immune system does not have the capacity to fight infections, we wear a mask when we go to places polluted with dust and smog. People who are allergic to certain kinds of food will avoid those items in their diet. Likewise, if we are spiritual seekers, we should stay away from circumstances that pull the mind downward. The mind's real strength is its ability to see goodness. Such people will see only the good in everything and will find lessons to learn from wicked characters. These characters reveal the sufferings that ultimately befall such people and will be our fate also if we model ourselves on them. Through their lives, they caution us not to follow in their footsteps. We should follow the lead, the blueprint of life laid out for us by good people. This will lead us to ultimate victory.

We should be careful of each step we take as long as the mind is not in our control. Later on, circumstances will no longer easily affect us. Once we understand spirituality and get the mind in our hands, we need not worry anymore. We will not collapse under the weight of circumstances. If we start driving after we learn how to drive, the chances are ninety per cent that we will reach home without any mishap. The one who hasn't learnt how to drive will reach the hospital. Likewise, if we lead a life based on dharmic principles, our lives will be peaceful. For this, we must avoid bad company. We should only remain friends with those who listen to satsang — the words of spiritual masters. This will help us to redeem and uplift our minds. Otherwise, the weak will be pulled down by circumstances. It can be compared to rolling a boulder up a mountain for many days, reaching the summit, but then taking merely a moment to push it back down the mountain.

Sītā as Our Model

Sītā is a symbol of the mind. The mind goes after sense-objects. In her mind arose the desire to own the golden deer[7]. When such a thought arose in her mind, Rāma, who is God, became distant from her mind. When God moved away, the mind lost its balance. She became like a mad woman, unable to recognize the good from the bad. She lost her power of discernment and aimed terrible and harsh words at Lakṣhmaṇa who tried to reason with her. Then, Lakṣhmaṇa, synonymous with discipline, also left her. Thus, she lost both God and discipline. Then, Sītā who represents the mind, was captured by Rāvaṇa representing the senses. When discipline was lost, the mind became a slave to the senses.

The minds of many spiritual practitioners can be compared to Sītā who desired the golden deer. Her desire took Sītā to Rāvaṇa's

---

[7] Rāvaṇa sent his uncle, a rākṣhasa named Mārīcha, to take the form of a golden deer to captivate Sītā's mind. Rāma went in search of the deer. Soon, Sītā also sent Lakṣhmaṇa away as she feared for Rāma's safety. In the absence of the two brothers Rāvaṇa was able to abduct Sītā.

prison. Even after learning the scriptures and listening to satsang, many do not let go of their attachments or desires. There are also those with the mind of Rāvaṇa. If we feel that we have been caught in the clutches of the rākṣhasa, taking the lead from Sītā, we should correct our mistakes through spiritual practices.

In Rāvaṇa's clutches, Sītā fixed her mind on Rāma with firm conviction and devotion. Her trust that Rāma would come and rescue her was absolute. This gave Sītā self-confidence and courage. Sītā made one mistake: she desired the golden deer — because the mind always chases behind desires. It was because Sītā's mind went after the golden deer, that Śhrī Rāma went far away from her, and Lakṣhmaṇa also left her. This led to Sītā being abducted by Rāvaṇa. Realizing her mistake, Sītā refused to even enter Rāvaṇa's palace. She did not heed the many temptations Rāvaṇa spread out in front of her. She was offered the role of his queen and promised many valuable gifts. Many of Rāvaṇa's maids were sent to advise Sītā in various ways to succumb to Rāvaṇa. They threatened and tried to scare her but to no avail. She sat in remorse under the overspread branches of a tree, impervious to the rain and heat, chanting "Rāma...Rāma...Rāma..." incessantly. Likewise, if we make mistakes, we should intend to correct them. Our mind can also get caught by such a rākṣhasa and taken captive by asuric (demonic) desires. We must gain liberation from them. Dedicated spiritual practice is the way forward. We should not allow the mind to wander like before. Even if we fail on the spiritual path, we should hold tight to the divine feet of the Lord. And we should also strive to redeem and uplift ourselves. Victory comes when both go together. When problems arise in our lives, we will try to blame others. We should know that no one else is to blame for our sorrow but ourselves.

Amma remembers an incident: once, a teacher asked his student, "Where is your homework?" The student answered, "Please forgive me, sir. The whole of yesterday evening, there was a big racket in my room. So, I was unable to do my homework." Hearing this, the surprised teacher asked, "What was this big noise that disturbed you the entire evening?" The student replied, "It was the noise from the T.V. It was so loud that I couldn't do my homework." The teacher enquired, "Why didn't you tell those who were watching it to turn the volume down?" Immediately, the student answered, "No sir, I couldn't do that." "But why?" enquired the teacher. The boy hung his head and answered, "There was no one else in the room, sir." We can understand a child behaving in this manner. But it is not right when grown-ups justify or cover up their faults by making excuses. We should take responsibility for our faults and try to make amends.

The mind can be calm and silent when we are in solitude. There will be no circumstances to alarm or upset the mind. If the same individual is able to maintain the same peace and discipline even in the midst of society, we can say that he has moved forward on the spiritual path. His peace of mind remains unbroken even amidst all the problems surrounding him. If he is able to stand firm in dharma even when faced with continuous challenges, we can say that he is established in dharma. Śhrī Rāma shows us such an example through his life. He had to constantly face intense challenges throughout his life. But he did not swerve even an inch from the path of dharma.

Testing the Quality of Our Integrity

Each obstacle and trial we face in life are, in fact, touchstones that test our character and the quality of our ideals. For Rāma, Sītā, and Bharata, the act of Kaikēyī blocking Rāma's coronation became the touchstone to test the quality of their integrity and precepts.

As Daśharatha's eldest son, Rāma was the rightful heir to the throne. Even Daśharatha does not have the right to deny him his birthright. Lakṣhmaṇa, Rāma's younger brother, requests Rāma to take dharmic action to claim his right to the throne and win over fate. It would have been dharmic if Rāma had taken this approach and won the kingdom for himself. But Rāma decided not just to follow the path of dharma, but also the path of greatness and sacrifice. He accepted the path of the highest dharma, not just common dharma.

Rāma could have accepted the kingdom later when Bharata pleaded with him, and when his guru Vasiṣhṭha asked him to do so. But Rāma had decided to stand true to a higher ideal — because Rāma thought of everyone's good. He knew that Bharata would be a skilful administrator. He had to save his father from the demerits of breaking his vow. Therefore, Rāma willingly chose the path of sacrifice and the welfare of all.

Now, let us look at Lakṣhmaṇa's decisions. When Rāma refused to follow his advice and take the crown by force, Lakṣhmaṇa could have remained in the palace. Instead, he acquiesced to his brother's decision and, in the role of a personal attendant, followed him to the forest.

What about Sītā? A forest is definitely not a safe place for women. Rāma asked her to remain in the palace. But Sītā also chose to follow her highest dharma.

The kingdom was given to Bharata by his father Daśharatha. Bharata's guru Vasiṣhṭha also asked him to accept the kingdom. So, if Bharata had accepted sovereignty over the throne of Ayōdhyā, none would blame him for doing so. But what did Bharata do? He approached his brother Rāma, who despite all his sincere entreaties, was determined not to accept the crown. So, Bharata took Rāma's pādukās and placed them on the throne. He also wore the rustic attire worn by Rāma and Lakṣhmaṇa and resided in a hut. He ruled the land as Rāma's representative. Thus, Bharata also accepted the highest form of dharma over and above ordinary, common dharma.

Bharata traveled with his army to the forest to bring Rāma back and crown him king. There is a story of Śhrī Rāma and the presiding deity of the forest, the Vanadēvatā, regarding this. The Vanadēvatā asks Śhrī Rāma how she can make life in the forest comfortable for him. Śhrī Rāma replies, "I have only one request to make. Remove the thorns from the path we have just traveled." The Vanadēvatā asks, "Lord! You have already reached here. So, what is the use of removing the thorns from the path you have already traveled?" Rāma replies, "My younger brother Bharata will walk barefoot through that forest path to come to me. His feet should not walk over thorns."

The deity of the forest asks Rāma, "Is your brother so weak and fragile that he cannot bear the pain of thorns under his feet?"

Rāma answers, "No. His body is diamond-hard. But when thorns pierce his feet, he will grieve that the same thorns would have pierced my feet. That is my fear. Already, he is very sad that I left Ayōdhyā and came to the forest. I do not wish to increase his sorrow."

Look at the depth of the love between the Lord and his devotee. The devotee only thinks of the Lord's well-being. As for the Lord, his attention is solely on the well-being of his devotee.

Rāma and Lakṣhmaṇa reacted differently when they heard that Bharata was traveling with his army through the forest. Lakṣhmaṇa saw Bharata and his army from afar. He thought that Bharata was coming to attack Rāma. He became furious. Often, we succumb to our anger without knowing the actual facts. A moment's patience and wise consideration will save us from making grave mistakes. This is why we say a gap between thought and action is needed. The light of awareness will enter that gap, and it will save us from serious blunders.

An incident comes to mind: a man was driving his car down a narrow road. The driver in front was going very slowly. The man honked his horn continuously, but the driver in front still would not make way for him to overtake. The man lost control over his mind and thought, "Just wait till we get to a wider road; I will teach him a lesson!"

Then, a small sticker pasted on the rear windshield of the car in front caught his attention, 'I am physically disabled. Please excuse me.'

Reading those words, the man suddenly calmed down. He patiently drove his car behind the other. When he reached home, he reflected, "Why do we need stickers to become patient towards others? There could be so many reasons for driving slowly — it would not be possible to write them all down and stick them to the windshield. If the driver had lost his job or lost a beloved relative due to death, that could also cause him to drive slowly. How can you write such things on a sticker? We will never know the trials and tribulations of others. Therefore, from today onwards, I will also respect invisible stickers." Thus, both the person who had accepted his disability and the one who had the patience to acknowledge it, were able to move forward together.

We need patience and forgiveness to enjoy life's beauty. Don't we respect others who show patience towards us? Who forgive us? We should also have the same patience and forgiveness towards others. We should see tough times as opportunities given by God to test the quality and worth of our minds.

Uproot the Latent Tendencies of the Mind

In the Vālmīki Rāmāyaṇa, Rāma was a human being equal to God. A man must be faithful to his three-fold dharma – as an individual, as part of a family, and to society. In Rāma's life, we can see the intensity of joy and the ferocity of sorrow that a human being has to experience in his life. Despite facing all the limitations of a human birth, Rāma and the Rāmāyaṇa teach us that dharma can be unfailingly performed.

When the war between Rāma and Rāvaṇa was nearing its end, Rāma cut off Rāvaṇa's heads, one by one. When one head fell, another came up in its place. Rāvaṇa's heads symbolize the endless desires that are born of ignorance. As long as we remain ignorant, our vāsanās – our latent desires and tendencies, will be never-ending. After a long and fierce battle, Rāma ends the war by shooting an arrow and piercing Rāvaṇa's heart. Likewise, if a sādhak, a spiritual seeker, tries to control his sense organs one by one, the effort will never have an end. We should aim for the root of our likes and dislikes, our anger and sorrow, etc. If we cut a tree branch, we will see four small branches sprouting in its place. Vāsanās are comparable to this phenomenon. Yet, if we uproot something, it will never sprout again. Change will happen only if we destroy ignorance. For this, we need a strong and determined sense of purpose.

Amma remembers a story: from his childhood onwards, a man was afraid of sleeping. He would spend sleepless nights, afraid that something was hiding under his bed. When the fear became uncontrollable, he went to a psychologist and said, "When I lie down to sleep, the thought of someone hiding underneath my bed overwhelms me; I become too scared to sleep. I feel that I am going mad." The psychologist replied, "If properly treated, this disease can be cured in a year. Come and see me thrice a week. I will cure you of your malady." The patient asked, "What is your fee?" The psychologist said, "It will be 2,000 rupees per sitting, and I may have to treat you for up to two hours per session." The patient said, "Let me think about it; I will get back to you." After many days, the psychologist met the man on the street and asked him, "You didn't come to me for your sessions; what is the reason?" The man replied, "You told me your fee was 2,000 rupees per sitting. So, I calculated my yearly fee at three sessions per week. I realized that it would add up to a huge sum. So, I found another way. There is a carpenter who lives in my neighborhood. I gave him 1,000 rupees. He cured my disease for 1,000 rupees. By saving the money I would have spent on your fees, I was able to buy a new car. Before, I spent sleepless nights, scared and sad. Now, I have no more fear or sorrow. I sleep well. And above all, I am thrilled because I could also buy a new car."

Hearing this, the psychologist asked anxiously, "How did the carpenter cure you?" "Oh! He sawed off the four legs of my bed. Now there is no space for anyone to come and hide underneath it; my fear has disappeared." What is the message of this story? Most of our problems arise from our delusions. If the delusion is removed, the problem is solved. A child fears ghosts inside a dark room. The best way to solve the problem is to light a lamp and drive away the darkness. Then, the child will be convinced that there are no ghosts in the room.

Likewise, if we can imbibe spiritual knowledge, all our problems will end. It is not enough to clear the weeds; they must be uprooted. Otherwise, they will come up again. Likewise, we must uproot our ignorance. This is not possible without the guidance of a Satguru. We must turn to the eternal and perfect God to find contentment. We must uplift ourselves to a state where we see the entire universe permeated with divinity. The Rāmāyaṇa opens up the way for us to attain this knowledge. The lessons imparted through the Rāmāyaṇa lead us to the path of eternal peace and bliss.

The Dharma of a King

The Rāmāyaṇa is the life story of Śhrī Rāmachandra. Rāma is the epitome of dharma, always truthful. He was a Jitēndra, one who has conquered his senses; he was humble, gentle, and fair in his speech; he was fearless and valiant; he was undefeated in war; he had mastered all the sciences and authoritative scriptures; he was handsome, with perfect features; and gladdened all hearts. The list of Rāma's noble qualities is unparallelled. He was always steadfast in his dharma. He never swerved from his dharma, even when faced with painful personal dilemmas. Rāma was always ready to renounce anything for dharma's sake.

Why did Rāma, the epitome of dharma, abandon Sītā? Such a question may indeed arise. The answer is that Rāma was a husband and a king. His dharma as a king took precedence over his dharma as an individual or his dharma to his family. The foremost priority of the king is the well-being of his subjects. The king is the lord of his subjects. Rāma insisted that his subjects should not harbor even a shadow of a doubt about their king. This was why Rāma gave such importance to the word of even a washerman. The king must demonstrate how dharma can remain strong in the land.

The washerman blamed Rāma for accepting back his wife, who had spent time as another man's prisoner. Rāma was very clear about his wife's fidelity. But, if a situation arose in which the subjects doubted the queen's purity, it would weaken his subjects' respect for dharma. A situation will arise in the land where men and women can justify their misdeeds. As a king, Rāma was determined to never be a wrong role model for others. This was the reason why, although it gave him unbearable pain to part from her, Rāma sent Sītā to the forest.

Through this gesture, Rāma also fulfilled Sītā's desire. The custom of fulfilling a pregnant woman's desires is prevalent even now. There is a custom in which the wife's family comes and takes her back to her family home for the remainder of her pregnancy. During this time, the woman should remain happy, without anything to trouble her. We should be careful to speak words that give her joy and give her all the food she desires. Her mind should always remain sattvic, listening to stories and hymns of God. A child is growing within her as a part of her body. The mother's thoughts and emotions shape the child's mind. The story of Prahlāda illustrates this.[8] Sītā gratefully remembered spending time in many āśhrams during their exile in the forest. She desired to stay in an āśhram and remain joyful and content during her pregnancy.

Dharma to our country takes precedence over our dharma as an individual. A military officer who has gone on leave to spend time with his wife and son may be immediately recalled due to an unexpected outbreak of hostilities. Should he stay back with his wife and son or go to war? Safety for people and homes is possible only if a free nation exists. So, even a soldier should consider his country first, and his wife and son should not take priority over his country. Therefore, what option did Rāma, the epitome of dharma, have at this juncture? Rāma knows Sītā well. Yet, he is also determined

[8] The Purāṇas attribute the young boy Prahlāda's unwavering devotion to stemming from his mother's devotional practices, which he is said to have absorbed while in her womb.

that not even a shadow of doubt should exist in people's minds regarding their king and queen.

Rāma demonstrates here the care and awareness that has to be ever-present for people in places of authority. The most important duty of a king is the welfare of his subjects. His dharma as a king is paramount. The country's interests are paramount when holding a position of power, whether as the prime minister or chief minister. It takes precedence over mother, wife, and children. This is the precedent, the ideal shown by Rāma. It may seem like neglect or even ill-treatment. Rāma shows through his own life that such problems may arise while governing a country. He does not say in words how an ideal ruler should behave; he always lives true to the noblest ideals.

Others think that Rāma abandoned a pregnant Sītā. Rāma can never abandon Sītā. Their relationship is such that Sītā always resides in Rāma's heart. Likewise, Rāma's place was in Sītā's heart. None could separate them. More than anyone, Sītā knew that Rāma was the epitome of dharma. The kings of yore could marry as many times as they wanted. But even during a yajña requiring the presence of the queen,

Rāma did not even think of another woman to take his wife's place. When it became clear that the yajña could not be performed without his wife's presence, a golden statue of Sītā was kept in her place.

Just as Sītā desired, she was able to spend her pregnancy and give birth to her children in Vālmīki's āśhram. The wife supports her husband in the performance of his dharma. Sītā was such a wife.

Rulers should invariably be role models. They should always stand firm on the side of dharma. No one should be able to perform a misdeed by taking their example. It is said, "Yathā rājā, tathā prajā." — "As the king is, so are the subjects." His subjects will emulate the king. Therefore, the king should be very aware of each of his words and actions.

Haven't we seen children imitating Amma here in the Amritapuri āśhram? For Amma, her children are God, so when Amma comes on stage, she raises her hands in prayer to her children. Before she sits on her seat, she will touch it with reverence and pray. It is the seat that gives us the space to sit. Amma gently touches the seat and prays to the earth. We should be ever grateful to this earth. Then Amma will prostrate. Only afterwards does Amma take her seat. Through her actions, she is demonstrating the principle of respect and thankfulness for everything. Seeing this, before they sit, Amma's children also raise their hands in prayer to everyone. From this, we can understand that they imitate what we show them.

Family Bonds Founded on Sacrifice

Rāma knew about the boons demanded by Kaikēyī on the eve of his coronation as crown prince. According to kingly tradition, as the eldest son of Daśharatha, Rāma was entitled to the throne. Yet, solely to honor his father's promise to Kaikēyī, Rāma prepared to leave for the forest. In today's world, according to the latest management principles, many may think that Rāma should not have gone into exile. Daśharatha also said, "Rāma, do not leave for the forest; I shall face the consequences myself."

But Rāma stood firm in his decision. He believed that as a son, he was duty-bound to remain faithful to his father's promises. He knew that the gates of hell would open for his father if he broke his word. His father should go to heaven, not hell. His father should not bow his head before anyone for Rāma's sake. Rāma proves this point through his actions as he willingly undergoes great sacrifices. This fidelity to his dharma ultimately prepares the way for the rākṣhasa Rāvaṇa's destruction.

Rāma's face did not express any special joy when the news of his coronation was broken to him; neither was he sad when he realized that he had lost his kingdom and was exiled to the forest. But upon hearing this news, Lakṣhmaṇa blazed up in anger. A calm Rāma consoled and pacified him. Even Kaikēyī's own son Bharata could not tolerate his mother's ruthless desires. Bharata went to the forest, seeking Rāma to bring him back and give the throne of Ayōdhyā to him. The dialogue that ensues between Bharata and Rāma is among the most touching scenes in the Rāmāyaṇa.

Bharata knew that his brother towered over him in stature, in knowledge, age, and nobility. So, he categorically refused to sit on the throne. He was ready to fast unto death to make Rāma accept the throne. Yet Rāma would not flinch even an inch from his decision. Seeing the brothers' love and respect for each other, those who witnessed their meeting in the forest became teary-eyed. Finally, Bharata bowed down to Rāma's will. He became ready to rule the kingdom as Rāma's representative.

While Lakṣhmaṇa physically accompanied Rāma as he journeyed through the forests,

Bharata stayed back in Ayōdhyā, with his mind constantly immersed in Rāma.

He served the world but lived in constant fidelity to the highest spiritual principle — never letting Rāma out of his heart, never forgetting him even for a moment. Thus, Bharata could emulate Rāma's noble life and live according to his elder brother's ideals.

Bharata entirely renounced his sense of doership as he ruled the kingdom as Śhrī Rāma's or God's representative. It was Rāma himself who ruled the kingdom. By meditating on Rāma, Bharata became Rāma. It is the state when the Lord and his devotee become one. The water in a river creates two shores. If the water dries up, there are no longer two shores, no near or far. The guru and disciple seem to be two, but in reality, there is only one. When the disciple's ego disappears, then there is no more duality. When the disciple attains total surrender, the guru acts through the disciple. This is why the disciple performs disciplined spiritual practice based on the yamas and niyamas — the restraints and observances, the moral codes of spiritual practices.

This brings to mind the story of two modern-day brothers: two brothers were in the business of selling vegetables. The elder one noticed that his younger sibling would, once in a while, steal from the shop. He wanted to catch him red-handed and said, "I won't be here for a week as I am leaving for Mumbai." The younger brother nodded his head. In reality, the elder brother had no plan to visit Mumbai. The younger one decided to use this opportunity and brought some banana bunches from the shop home with him. The very next night, the elder brother knocked on his brother's door. As the door opened, he saw the stolen banana bunches inside the room. As soon as the younger brother saw his elder sibling, he angrily said, "If you are a human being, you should at least to some degree be honest. When you left, you told me that you would be away for a week. Why did you return today itself?" In this incident, the younger brother, who had committed the theft, blames his older brother. Only such a bond exists between brothers in this day and age.

Daśharatha's sons were not like these brothers. They were ready to give way to the other and to uphold dharma. This is why we have much to learn from all four of them.

We also have many lessons to learn from Kaikēyī and Mantharā, and should take care not to emulate their wrong decisions and actions. It can be said that we received the Rāmāyaṇa only because Kaikēyī listened to Mantharā's false words. Many of us were able to learn many lessons because of their wrongdoing. We should not hate the person who does wrong; on the contrary, we should allow them to atone for and correct their wrong deeds. Even while others were furious at Kaikēyī, who had committed an unpardonable wrong against Rāma, Rāma forbade them from speaking angrily to her. Rāma had no anger against anyone. He concentrated exclusively on performing his dharma.

Daśharatha never even once asked Rāma to go to the forest or to hand over the kingdom to Bharata. He told Rāma, "Imprison me and rule the country." But Rāma knew, that was not the path of dharma. He wanted to fulfill his father's words — the promise Daśharatha had once given to Kaikēyī. There should never be any obstacle to their fulfillment. So, Rāma left for the forest to uphold the truth of his father's words. These are the words he spoke to Lakṣhmaṇa, who was blazing with anger when Kaikēyī forbade Rāma's coronation: "I know that you love me, hence this emotion. Yet, we must uphold our father's promise. It is not proper for you to display such anger." Śhrī Rāma calms and consoles Lakṣhmaṇa with these words of tender love. He praises his brother's anger, acknowledging that it was not selfishness but love for Rāma that brought forth such unmitigated anger, and he also rebukes Lakṣhmaṇa with words of tenderness. This clearly shows Rāma's statesmanship and deep knowledge of life's realities.

Rāma Rājya

Sacrifice and an expansive vision can be seen throughout Rāma's life. Rāma returned after his exile and took up the reins of the kingdom only to honor his word given to Bharata. Rāma ruled the kingdom in order to educate the world on how to be an ideal ruler. A ruler has no kith or kin. He has only his subjects. The exclusive goal of the king is the welfare of his subjects. Ruling the kingdom is a tapas — a one-pointed spiritual discipline. For an ideal ruler, it is God's worship. It is dedicating and surrendering one's own self to the world. Rāma ruled with such surrender. He renounced his likes and dislikes to uphold his dharma as a king. He even renounced Sītā. Finally, he also let go of Lakṣhmaṇa.

His rule was truly auspicious, and the land was prosperous. As the king was established in dharma, the subjects also lived true to dharma. Rāma Rājya is famous worldwide as a synonym for ideal rule. Amma remembers an incident: an assembly of poets was being held in the court of King Bhōja. A poet sang in praise of King Bhōja, saying he was equal to King Rāma and his kingdom equalled Rāma Rājya. Hearing this, everyone applauded. A crow flying across the assembly pooped on the poet who had sung the king's praises. The poet became upset, and the king ordered the crow to be caught in a net.

The crow spoke, "O king! There is no need to catch me in a net. I pooped on this poet's head because he was lying. You are not equal to Rāma, neither is your kingdom, Rāma Rājya. I shall prove this to you." The crow continued, "Please accompany me with your ministers and this poet." So the king, his ministers, and the poet accompanied the crow. The crow reached a cave's entrance; they all went inside. Inside, they saw mud heaped up. The crow asked them to remove the mud heap. They did so, and a hoard of gleaming jewels lay revealed. The crow said, "These jewels belong to Rāma's time. A rich man with no children prayed that he would gift the king a pot of jewels if he begot children. With God's grace, a child was born to the rich man. He reached Rāma's presence with the pot of jewels.

However, Rāma refused to accept the jewels without just reason. He ordered that the jewels be distributed amongst the needy in the kingdom. But there were no poor people in Rāma Rājya. Rāma told the rich man to gift the jewels to anyone who desired them. But not a single person in the Kingdom of Rāma wanted to accept the jewels without toiling and earning them with their labor.

These jewels have lain here since then, as no one was willing to accept them." The crow continued, "O king! Look carefully; you will see that all your ministers and the poet have closed fists. Command them to open their fists." As they opened them, the king saw their hands full of jewels. "As I was talking, they were gathering jewels. This was why they kept their fists closed. I hope you understand now why I said that your kingdom is in no way equal to Rāma Rājya."

Bharata decided he did not want the kingdom rejected by his elder brother, whom he found to be equal to God. He traveled to the forest to bring Śhrī Rāma back immediately. He fell at Śhrī Rāmachandra's feet and, with tears in his eyes, implored him to return, and take up the responsibility and burden of ruling the kingdom. "Come back with me and rule the kingdom," he prays to Śhrī Rāmachandra.

Śhrī Rāma, pleased with his younger brother's love and devotion, embraces him with tender affection, wipes away his tears, and consoles him. With love, Rāma enquires about the well-being of his subjects, including Kaikēyī, who was the reason for his exile.

The foundational principles of the noble vision of Rāma Rājya are based on the questions that he, subsequently, asks Bharata. Śhrī Rāma tenderly enquires of Bharata saying,

"I hope you are ruling the kingdom with focused awareness, wisdom, and self-control. I hope that you are attentive to every aspect of kingship."

"Are you giving due respect and adoration to the knowledgeable ones, the forefathers, servants, preceptors, those who are equal to your father, and old men?"

"Have you kept men of courage and wisdom, who have gained control over their senses, as your ministers?"

"Young one, I hope you are not enslaved by sleep."

Śhrī Rāma continues, "Are you working with energy, enthusiasm, and awareness?"

"As night ends, do you reflect upon all that has to be achieved during the day?"

"I trust that you do not make unilateral decisions on matters of governance; at the same time, I hope that you take the counsel of only a few people so that your decisions do not become the talk of the marketplace.

"I hope you are prompt in starting small enterprises that will lead to steady and sustainable development."

Śhrī Rāma continues, "I hope the other kings know of your actions only after you have achieved your goals, or are on the verge of completing them."

"I hope that you accept the counsel of one intelligent, wise, and knowledgeable person rather than a thousand unintelligent ones."

"Remember that even if you have tens of thousands of men, they will not fittingly support you if they have no wisdom and discernment. Have you given due honor and respect to the youth, battle strategists, those who have proved their mettle, and the valiant ones?"

Rāma asks Bharata, "Are you giving the army their rations and salaries on time? I hope you do not delay in giving them what is their due. My brother, if they do not receive their food and salary on time, they will become angry with the rulers and wreak vengeance."

"Have you kept as your messenger a scholar who is capable and brilliant, stands for the truth, and is born in our kingdom?"

"Do you pay due respect to the Chārvāka[9] pundits? Do not forget that though they are ignorant of the ultimate truth; they can create mischief and unrest."

"Perform adoration of the divine (ārādhanā), ritualistic worship (pūjā), fulfill all ordained duties, and celebrate all festivals without fail."

"You must see that the fields are plowed well and the seeds sown on time. It would be best if you gave special encouragement and consideration to the farmers. Agriculture and cow rearing give comfort and are necessary for everyone's well-being. It is the villages that provide the food to satiate our hunger."

"It is the food produced by the farmers in the villages that feed the towns. So, they should be well supported."

"I hope you protect the ponds, rivers, streams, canals, and cattle well."

---

[9] Refers to the materialists of ancient India, a school of philosophy that regards sensory experience alone as a valid source of knowledge.

"Are you providing whatever is needed by small businessmen and prominent entrepreneurs? I hope you are giving them adequate protection."

"I hope sufficient measures are taken to safeguard women and that they are protected and consoled when needed."

"Are you protecting the trees and forests?"

"I hope the inflow of money is much greater than the expenses incurred."

"Are you spending the money in the treasury wisely and for the upkeep of goodness? Do you interact well with your subjects and try to understand their problems personally?

"Did you establish good relations with the neighboring kingdoms?"

Śhrī Rāma said many such things and gave Bharata comprehensive advice on all the steps to be taken by the ruler or king for the country's sustainable development and its citizens' well-being, prosperity, and happiness. Even after listening to these words from his elder brother, Bharata prayed to Rāma to return and take up the reins of the kingdom.

But Rāma stood firm and said that he is bound to keep the promise he had given to his father, and that he will not swerve from his dharma. Finally, Bharata had to agree to rule the kingdom as Śhrī Rāma's representative. With great reverence, Bharata placed Rāma's pādukās (sandals) on his head and returned to Ayōdhyā. He then placed Rāma's pādukās on the throne and, with love and adoration for his elder brother, lived a life of renunciation.

He renounced all kingly pleasures and subsisted on fruits and nuts, staying true to the life of Śhrī Rāma in the forest. He slept on the floor, constantly meditating upon Śhrī Rāma, and lived a spartan life. Obeying Śhrī Rāma's advice, he ruled the land with the happiness and prosperity of his subjects foremost in his mind.

A ruler is only the people's representative. The ruler's authority and strength are vested in the people's hands. Therefore, rulers are bound one hundred percent to fulfilling the promises and guarantees they have given to the people. Above all, the ruler is God's representative. Everything in this universe comes under God's jurisdiction.

God is the supreme authority. Therefore, rulers should not rule according to their whims and fancies; they should respect the people's will and rule with humility. Real rulers are humble servants of the people. They are not enslaved by their ego and serve with humility even while in a position of great authority. They should lead simple lives; sacrifice and selfless service should be their life vows. A good ruler should not become intimate with only a few and keep others at a distance. He should not give excessive favors to the ones close to him and bring down or ignore others.

In short, a good ruler should have equal vision to a large extent. If a ruler feels greater liking and closeness to just a few people, it will adversely affect the majority. This is why it is said that a noble ruler should be a good sannyāsi – a monk who has renounced his own desires, within. This is what Bharata's life teaches us.

Rāma also shows us how to live without renouncing truth and dharma, even when he was enmeshed in life's challenges and experienced deep pain.

Rāma was not just the epitome of dharma; he was an ideal leader whose practical intelligence and skill in action were unrivaled. The first task of a leader is to awaken self-confidence in his followers. Vibhīṣhaṇa was addressed as "Laṅkēśha" — the Lord of Laṅka, by Rāma when he took refuge in Rāma. Not only that, but even before the war started, Rāma crowned Vibhīṣhaṇa as the King of Laṅka.

Through this act, Rāma sends a clear message to everyone: Rāvaṇa may be the King of Laṅka now, but Vibhīṣhaṇa will soon ascend to the throne. Through this act, Rāma infused his army with the self-confidence and courage needed to battle against Rāvaṇa's army. This proves that Rāma was far-sighted — another indispensable quality of a true leader.

Another quality needed for a leader is to have faith and belief in those who stand with him. A good leader should recognize the capabilities of their followers and assign suitable tasks for them. Rāma chose Hanumān as his emissary to send his own message to Sītā. He chose Aṅgada to warn Rāvaṇa. He gave Nala the responsibility of building a bridge across the ocean to Laṅka. A good leader should not take responsibility for doing everything himself. He should know the art of delegation.

Another quality of a good leader is the ability to keep a clear goal in front of his supporters.

Śhrī Rāma made it very clear to the Vānaras[10] that going to Laṅka and bringing Sītā back was the goal. If the goal is clear, it will inspire everyone to take effective action.

Another essential quality for a great leader is magnanimity. When Vibhīṣhaṇa sought asylum with Rāma, Rāma debated the matter with his Vānara ministers. They were of the opinion that Vibhīṣhaṇa was, to all intents and purposes, a spy, and that giving him refuge was dangerous. But Śhrī Rāma replied, "I will protect all those who take refuge in me, even if it is Rāvaṇa himself."

Śhrī Rāma convinced the Vānara leaders of the great advantage of having Vibhīṣhaṇa on their side in the battle against Rāvaṇa. A leader must engage with his colleagues to discuss matters and hear their perspectives.

Yet another quality necessary for every leader is the equanimity of mind that characterized Rāma even in adverse circumstances. When we manage a company with five hundred

---

[10] Literally 'monkeys' in Sanskrit, Vānaras are beings with ape-like features who with their exceptional intelligence and strength play a pivotal role in the Rāmāyaṇa as faithful servants of Lord Rāma.

employees, we manage five hundred minds. Only if the leader has his own mind under his control can he effectively manage the minds of others. Otherwise, the organization is more inclined to fail or fall into danger.

When we hear the name Rāvaṇa, a ten-headed rākṣhasa image comes to mind. The ten heads symbolize Rāvaṇa's extraordinary brilliance. Rāvaṇa had the intelligence of ten people combined or even more; this is what it signifies. But even though he was a brilliant rākṣhasa, his mind was impure. He was a puppet in the hands of his own desires. It was easy for Rāma, who had conquered his sense organs, to defeat Rāvaṇa. A leader must never be enslaved by his sense organs; he should be a jitēndriya[11].

Rāma is the ideal model for all those who desire to become a leader. By studying Rāma's life, they will receive all the necessary knowledge.

[11] 'Someone who has conquered his senses' — composed of 'jit' meaning 'conquered' or 'subdued', and 'indriya' meaning 'senses' or 'sense organs.' Jitēndra is a variant spelling that is a popular first name.

Seeing With the Proper Perspective

Amma recalls an incident that happened during the war between Rāma and Rāvaṇa: Rāma, Lakṣhmaṇa, and all their warriors fell into a swoon when Rāvaṇa's son Indrajit released his celestial arrow, the nāgāstra. Sensing that his Lord was in danger, the celestial bird Garuḍa flew down to the battlefield. His mere presence nullified the effect of the nāgāstra, and Rāma and Lakṣhmaṇa were saved from danger.

Suddenly, a thought arose in Garuḍa's mind, "Until now, I had thought that Rāma was God. But now, only my help released him from the clutches of the arrow. Then how can Rāma be God?" As this thought unsettled him, Garuḍa went to Sage Nārada and laid bare the doubts that plagued his mind. Nārada said, "There is a crow named Kākabhuśhuṇḍi. Go to him and become his disciple. Your problem will be solved."

Hearing Nārada's reply, Garuḍa thought, "How can I, the King of Birds, become the disciple of a mere crow?" But, as Nārada advised, he approached Kākabhuśhuṇḍi and shared his doubt with the crow. Kākabhuśhuṇḍi replied, "You are a fool. The all-powerful Lord allowed you an opportunity to serve him. You cannot even lift your wings without his grace. Rāma veiled his own strength to allow you to serve him. This is his unbounded grace. Know this and bow down in reverence to him." Garuḍa's ego left him as he heard the wise words of Kākabhuśhuṇḍi. He prostrated before Rāma and begged forgiveness. Thus, Garuḍa was freed from his ignorance. Even though an incarnation, Rāma behaved like a human being to become an ideal for ordinary humans to aspire to.

For example, how will humanity accept God if he incarnates as a tiger? If we go in a police uniform to catch a thief, the miscreant will undoubtedly run away. You need to put on the clothes of a thief and become one among them to easily catch them. Likewise, humans can be inspired and uplifted only if God descends to their level. It is difficult to make ornaments out of pure gold. We need to add some copper to it. Likewise, God descends among humanity, manifesting the characteristics of a human being.

When Amma was a young girl, she would go to cut grass for the cows. There was a traditional healer who knew about the value of medicinal herbs as a home cure. On certain days, he would also come to collect some medicinal grasses. He would pluck Vaṭṭakudaṅgaḷ, Kaiyyōnni, Karuka, and many other kinds of grasses that were medicinal. They were just plain grass for someone cutting grass for the cows. But in the eyes of the Āyurvēdic healer, they had high medicinal value. Only a traditional healer would know this. Likewise, to know the incarnations living amidst other humans, we need a particular saṁskāra — mental refinement.

If we see a stone, the stonecutter who makes grinding stones will visualize a grinding stone in it. Someone who makes mortars will visualize chiseling a mortar out of the stone. Those who make stone steps will say the stone is suitable for making steps. A sculptor will see the vigraha (form) of Dēvī, the Divine Mother, in it. Everyone sees the stone according to their perspective. So, it is our outlook that should change. Today, we have sight, but we do not have the proper perspective.

Sumitrā says the most crucial verse in the Rāmāyaṇa. She gives advice to her son Lakṣhmaṇa, who is preparing to travel with his elder brother Rāma, who has been exiled to the forest. Sumitrā tells her son to see Rāma as his own father Daśharatha, to see Sītā as his mother, and the forest as Ayōdhyā, and to go in peace.

There is nothing wrong in considering this to be the most crucial verse in the Rāmāyaṇa. It shows the attitude to be maintained towards your elder brother, his wife, and those near you. It shows the attitude to be maintained towards the earth we live on and towards our surroundings. It shows how we should tackle the different situations that arise in life. All these three factors are dealt with in this one verse. This verse is a message for Lakṣhmaṇa as he treads the forest path, and for everyone on their life's journey. The verse speaks to us of devotion to the mother and father, to brothers and preceptors, devotion to the motherland, and respect and honor for women.

The meaning of this verse has been interpreted in various ways. Our life is fulfilled if we see the people around us as God. Likewise, we should be able to consider wherever we live akin to our own land. In reality, nothing is separate from us and no one is a stranger to us. *Vasudhaiva kuṭumbakam* — the whole world as one family — is our conviction, our ideal. The one divine consciousness is the essence of all. This is the in-depth meaning of this verse. In short, Bhārat's saṁskāra is encapsulated in these four lines, as if within a mother of pearl.

Even those circumstances that we find sorrowful may ultimately be for our benefit. This secret is revealed by Rāma's exile to the forest. When Rāma left for the forest, Kausalyā and Daśharatha were distraught, weighed down by sorrow. All the people of Ayōdhyā were gripped by grief; but the dēvas (celestial beings) and the hermits and sages of the forest exulted. They knew his stay in the forest was for the greater good and would lead to many reforms. Often, this is the truth about the sorrows and difficulties that beset our lives. We have a minimal understanding of it, as we do not know the impact of our actions performed in many previous lives, or what the future holds in store for us. Our understanding of events is based on the dim light shed by the present moment. This is how we label something as good or bad. But the reality will be far from what we assume. If we are able to change our attitudes and viewpoints, we will see our sorrows turning into blessings. This is why the guru tells us to maintain an equal vision and an attitude of acceptance. This does not mean that we should not become happy or that we should always remain unemotional. On the contrary, it means we should see the good and God's blessing in everything. We should accept everything as prasād — a divine gift from God. Throughout their lives, Rāma and Sītā manifest these qualities. An unrestrained ego and selfishness are the cause of all our sorrow. Rāma enthroned dharma over these. This is our responsibility also. This is the core of spirituality.

There is exceptional strength to stories and advice that contain goodness. Even if we do not make any particular attempt to live by the lessons they impart, through constant listening, they enter deep within us and merge into our minds and our saṁskāra, refining our mental impressions. They cleanse us and transform our lives. This is why we should read great and noble books like the Rāmāyaṇa and retell them to our children.

Where There Is Love, There Are No Obstacles

Sītā is Rāma's shadow. Wherever Rāma goes, Sītā goes along with him. The hardship of life in the forest did not affect Sītā at all. For her, there was no feeling of hardship. There is no hardship in love. On the contrary, we get the strength to forgive and forbear. It is love for her unborn child that gives a pregnant woman the strength to forbear, forgive, and forget. Mothers tolerate the insistent demands of their small children due to their love for them. A mother does not consider it a sacrifice because of her love for her child.

Most of us know the story of the milkmaid in Śhivājī's[12] palace-fortress: the woman had come up the hill to the fortress to sell milk, but by the time she was ready to return home, the fortress's gates had been closed for the night. Frightened, she begged the guards to open the gate for her as she had left her tiny baby, whom she was still breastfeeding, at home. She became

[12] Śhivājī Śhahajī Bhōnsalē, 1630 – 1680, King of the Marāṭha Empire.

crazed with anxiety, thinking of her baby alone at home. She went to each gate and pleaded with the guards, but no one heeded her request. The fortress within which the palace was situated was on top of a hill that rose to a very great height. There was no way to get out.

The milkmaid became distraught, like a mad woman. “My baby is alone; there is no one with her; I need to feed her!” These thoughts consumed her, and finally, she lost her presence of mind. Her only thought was her child. She jumped off the steep fortress wall and rolled over and over on the ground. Her body was torn and bleeding from thorns and stones. She did not realize any of this as she went home and fed her child. Everyone was shocked when she returned to the palace the next day. Greatly concerned, the king’s soldiers questioned her: “Yesterday, you were not allowed outside the gates. How did you get out?” They feared a breach in their security. If there was one, enemies could also get in through the breach in the walls and kill their king. They searched the entire area looking for an opening. They could find none and finally asked the woman herself.

She said, "I don't know, I jumped down from somewhere."

After searching for a long time, they found the place where she had jumped. No one could believe their eyes. It would be difficult to make it alive if anyone jumped from there. The soldiers asked the woman, "Can you jump from here again?" But she was afraid as she looked down from the height from which she had jumped the previous evening. Her entire body trembled as she refused to attempt it.

When the face of her crying infant was uppermost in her mind, she had no hesitation in jumping down the previous night. She was not afraid of death. She did not feel the pain when the stones and thorns cut her, and she bled all over. Her overwhelming love for the child consumed every other emotion. She did not find anything as a hardship. In love, you find the strength to forget and forgive everything.

When the full moon rises in the sky, the earth's water also rises. This is the time of high tide. Love will rise within us when we gain real awareness of our goal. Then, no power can turn us away from the goal.

The Relationship Between Guru and Disciple

There are many inspiring characters in the Rāmāyaṇa. One of the most magnificent characters is Hanumān. Hanumān is also the foremost devotee of Rāma. Hanumān's courage, enthusiasm, scholarship, discernment, and wisdom are unequaled. Even so, Hanumān does not have an iota of the 'I' feeling. He offered his body, mind, and unrivaled strength to Rāma. When in the service of Rāma, Hanumān forgets even the word 'rest.' It is believed that Hanumān lives forever as a chirañjīvī[13], to chant Lord Rāma's name and to hear Rāma's stories.

An incident in Hanumān's life illustrates the fundamental nature of the bond between the guru and the disciple. Once, a sage waded into the river and collected a palmful of water to

---

[13] One of the 'immortals' who remain embodied on earth until the end of the present age of unrighteousness. Depending on the source, seven to nine individuals are mentioned to belong to this class of being.

perform his evening worship. A gandharva[14], flying through the air, spat down, and the spittle fell into the water cupped in the open palms of the sage. The sage was both sad and angry. He went to Rāma and pleaded with him to uphold justice by executing the gandharva who had insulted him. Rāma agreed. Hearing about his impending death, the gandharva took refuge in Hanumān's mother Añjanā. Crying, he implored her, "Mother, I am in grave danger. You must save me. Give me your word." Añjanā's motherly heart could not refuse his request. She told Hanumān, "Son, I have given my word to save this gandharva's life. Make my word come true." Hanumān agreed to fulfill Añjanā's promise.

When Rāma arrived, Hanumān asked the gandharva to stand behind him and chant Rāma's name. Hanumān also stood with palms folded in prayer, chanting Rāma's name. All the arrows Rāma shot in the gandharva's direction returned and fell as flowers at Rāma's feet. Not even a single arrow pierced the gandharva. Hanumān and the gandharva continued to

[14] Gandharvas are a class of celestial beings who are musicians, singers, and dancers who entertain the dēvas or gods in heaven.

chant Rāma's name. Finally, Hanumān humbly prays to Rāma, "O Lord! If you allow it, the gandharva will ask for the sage's pardon." Śhrī Rāma and the sage agreed to the request and settled the dispute. The gandharva no longer had to fear for his life.

Hanumān's mother gave her word to the gandharva without knowing anything about him. But Śhrī Rāma was a knower of the past, present, and future. So, it would be natural for Hanumān to wonder why Rāma had committed to the sage's request. But Hanumān did not think like this. Even when he had to confront Rāma, he did so by taking refuge in Rāma and the Rāma mantra. He also led others to the path of devotion to Rāma. Hanumān shows us the supreme dharma of the disciple towards his master. His devotion to Rāma was not in the slightest bit shaken. The greatness of his devotion to Rāma saved the gandharva's life. Maybe all this was Bhagavān's līlā — the Lord's divine play, designed to measure Hanumān's devotion. Whatever the reason, Hanumān, as the ideal disciple, remains unrivaled.

We saw how Rāma, Sītā, Lakṣhmaṇa, and Bharata responded to life's challenges. They did not meekly accept all that came their way. They reflected on their dharma in each situation and endeavored to act accordingly. Likewise, Hanumān also acted with courage and discernment in each situation, foregoing ease and comfort. All of them gave great importance to human effort. Even so, there is one thing we should understand. Ultimately, only God's will prevails. Each one of us is only an instrument in God's hands.

A scene from the Sundara Kāṇḍa in the Rāmāyaṇa comes to mind. Hanumān reached Laṅka, and at the same time, a rākṣhasī (demoness) named Trijaṭā dreamt that a monkey had set Laṅka in flames. She shared this dream with her friends. Hanumān, who had concealed himself on a tree branch, listens to their conversation and thinks, "Bhagavān (Lord Rāma) only told me to give a message to Sītā; he did not ask me to set fire to Laṅka." But soon, Hanumān is in the hands of the rākṣhasas, and they take him to Rāvaṇa's court. Rāvaṇa orders his commander to tie cloth around Hanumān's tail, pour ghee on the cloth and then set it on fire. It was then that Hanumān understood that if Śhrī Rāma wanted something done, it could be accomplished even through his enemy Rāvaṇa. Many of us think, "What would have happened if I had not been there?" In reality, we are only instruments in the Lord's hands. He makes us act. The action bears perfect fruit when divine grace is combined with human effort.

Hanumān is the ideal example of strength and humility. He knew well when to use his strength and when to show humility. Hanumān would always introduce himself as Śhrī Rāma's servant.

When Hanumān meets Sītā for the very first time in the Aśhōkavana, the forest grove where Sītā is held captive by Rāvaṇa, he tells her that Rāma will cross over the ocean soon with his army of monkeys and rescue Sītā. Hearing this, Sītā becomes thoughtful. She shares her anxiety with him: "Will it be possible for an army of monkeys to fight against the mighty force of Rāvaṇa's army?" Hanumān showed his strength only to release Sītā from her fear. There is a beautiful message embedded in this incident. Usually, people scare others with their strength. But Hanumān showed his strength to ward off Sītā's fear.

A Vehicle of Our Culture

The Adhyātma Rāmāyaṇa Kiḷippaṭṭu is the version of the Rāmāyaṇa that is widespread and popular in Kerala. It is written as advice given by Lord Śhiva to Pārvatī Dēvī. Who is Śhiva? Śhiva is the head of a family. He is a father. He is the Lord of the Universe. Pārvatī Dēvī is also the head of her family. She is a mother. She is the Mother of the Universe. Pārvatī Dēvī, in the role of the disciple, absorbs the core principles of spirituality and dharma from her husband.

Likewise, in each family, the parents should talk about godly matters. Children should grow up in such an atmosphere. We should regain such a saṁskāra. Then, love will fill our homes; there will be unity and prosperity. Peace and a life based on right values will dawn in society.

A society will not save itself through principles confined to books and classroom teachings without any relation to life. Today, we are becoming isolated islands.

Suppose there is one car in a household. The son wants to go for a game of cricket, while the father wants to go to his club. The mother needs to go to the supermarket. Neither the father nor the son nor the mother were ready to concede to the others. Finally, what started as fiery words ended in a full-blown fight. Nobody left the house; instead, all three retreated to separate rooms and lay down. If they loved each other, the father could have dropped his son at the cricket ground, taken his wife to the supermarket, and then gone to the club. Then, they all would have been able to get what they wanted. But when they insisted that they needed the car for themselves, none of the three could get what they wanted, and it ended in harsh words and a family fight.

None of us are isolated islands; we are all links in a chain. If we unite, we can experience joy. But, as we alienate ourselves and split away, our minds will also become fragmented. Then, we will not be able to become dharmic or true even to ourselves. We are moving away from dharma. Looking back, we will feel ashamed to say that we have been born; we can never say that we have really lived. Even worms live better lives than us. They unite to procreate. They die. But they do not destroy the world. They do not give sorrow to others. Not only that, they serve nature in whatever way they can. This means that our lives are worse than that of worms. We say that we have intelligence and wisdom. But we grab everything for selfish pleasure and destroy nature as we go along. A worm shows more gratitude to this world than us. They only help nature; they do not harm it.

We say that we will never be a slave to anyone. But someone was needed to teach us how to tie our shoelaces. Didn't someone teach you how to cook? Didn't someone teach you how to sweep? How did you learn to study? How did you learn to eat food? We learn when someone teaches us or by watching others do it. When we are born, have we already learnt everything? No. We had an opportunity to learn each and every thing. Therefore, we should show our gratitude to all.

Everything is our guru, our teacher. Whatever we see is our guru. We have many things to learn, even from the tiny ant. We have lessons to learn from ants, snakes, birds, from everything. We get fruits and vegetables because the honey bee pollinates the plants. It also gives us honey. But what are we giving those tiny honey bees in return? The mother feeds and brings up her own child. But when the children are grown, what do they do to their mothers? Their only intention is to grab all their parents' wealth, even if they have to kill their mother and father. Today, most children give only sorrow to their parents.

This is the pattern of the life that we see around us. But it was not so in earlier days. The mother lived for the child, and the child for the mother. The father lived for the son, and the son lived for the father. They were established in dharma. Dharma came first and foremost in life.

In the place of dharma, we see selfishness. Everyone cares only for their own pleasure without any regard for anyone else. Mutual love is gone. This is why everyone is sad and full of tension. If this situation continues, the number of people with a mental health condition will increase in Bhārat, like in other countries. Today, each family member needs freedom. It has become rare for a family to watch a TV program together. Everyone wants to see what they like at that very moment. No one has the patience to wait until another has seen what they want. "You can watch your channel only after I watch mine;" these words may even lead to physical aggression.

No one is ready to forgive and forbear. The wife does not want the present husband; she wants a new one. So, she divorces him. The son does not want to live with his parents; he needs his freedom, and so leaves home. Maybe he will land in bad company. He may become addicted to drugs and other bad habits and finally end up in prison. Leaving home demanding "freedom, freedom" finally leads him to prison. This situation, prevalent in foreign countries, is now becoming common in Bhārat.

Children become addicted to drugs very fast and destroy their lives. They suffer from depression even over trivial matters. Many such children are unable to finish their studies. Their entire life is spent in sorrow and regret, giving sorrow to others also, enduring great suffering, and finally sliding down into thoughts of depression. The number of children who are ending their lives even at a young age is increasing. When Amma sees what is happening today, she feels that we should fear the misuse of drugs even more than war.

Blossoms, meant to spread their fragrance in this world, are now being infected with poison and drop off while they are still buds. The remedy for this is to promote and nourish the awareness of dharma. Therefore, even if their children do not like to hear it, parents should teach them the principles of dharma.

Small children may not like to brush their teeth, but their mothers will insist that they brush their teeth regularly, because only then will their teeth remain strong without any dental disease. Children should be made aware of spiritual principles in the form of stories and poems that entertain them. Through this, they will be aware of remaining faithful to dharma and not perform adharmic deeds. They will realize that they should not do anything that upsets their parents. They will feel that no one else should be hurt because of them. They will reflect on how to help others without bringing harm to anyone. Such knowledge should be given to children by their families. Parents should spend some time each day with their children, trying to instill such dharmic thoughts in them.

The Rāmāyaṇa is the vehicle of our culture. It is not merely moral advice. When we listen to, hear, and read the Rāmāyaṇa, a noble saṁskāra will unknowingly become strong within us. The Rāmāyaṇa has the power to do so. This is why it has been translated into many different languages and has profoundly influenced millions of hearts. This is why stories like the Rāmāyaṇa, and the history of human beings like Rāma — who were the pinnacles of dharma, should reach the younger generation through their parents and family members. Then, our lives as members of society will become meaningful.

The Rāmāyaṇa is a treasure trove of hymns of unparalleled beauty and exalted spiritual principles. When we read the Rāmāyaṇa, our devotion and knowledge will increase. In olden times, people read it with śhraddhā — faith and attention. The principles of the Rāmāyaṇa were reflected in their lives. The knowledge they received from spiritual books became their strength and gave relief to their minds as they struggled in life or faced extraordinary challenges. Nowadays, reading the Rāmāyaṇa has been reduced to a mere ritual. The children read it because the parents have read it. We can emulate the noble qualities that the Rāmāyaṇa presents before us only if we read it with discernment, and understand its inner meanings and spiritual principles. We cannot swim by reading a book on how to swim. Nowadays, everything has become a mere custom.

Amma remembers a story: there was a family who regularly performed pūjās (worship rituals). One day, when all the ingredients for the pūjā were set out, a cat came and drank the milk. The next day, when the cat came again to drink the milk kept aside for the pūjā, the father caught it and trapped it under an upside-down basket. Only then did he start the ritual. This became a habit; the cat would turn up to drink the milk, and the father would catch and confine it inside a basket.

After some time, the father died, and his son took over performing the pūjās. Emulating the father, he would also catch the cat and put it inside the basket. After a while, the cat died. So, the son started the pūjā only after fetching the neighbor's cat and keeping it closed inside a basket. The father had kept the cat inside a closed basket only because it drank the pūjā milk, but the son thought that it was a part of the pūjā rituals. This is how we are. We do not see the principles behind most of our traditions; we merely observe them. There are traditions that are still very relevant and others that are obsolete. We should be able to discern between the two.

We perform many actions without the proper knowledge. Such a situation also arises in the reading of the Rāmāyaṇa. This lack of knowledge is not limited to performing pūjās; every aspect of the spiritual traditions that Hindus follow has now become a mere ritual. We do not delve deep into its principles. So, we are unable to make our actions pure and sincere. Earlier, we could hear the Rāmāyaṇa and Bhāgavatam being read in many homes. Many people would come to listen. In those homes, both food and knowledge — annadāna and jñānadāna, are offered. A poor person is invited in, given food and dakṣhiṇā (a gift, usually in the form of money) as a symbol of seeing God in a human being, and the host prostrates in front of them. The core principle of Sanātana Dharma is to see the creator in creation. The sun does not need a candle. God does not need anything from us. The Rāmāyaṇa teaches us to see, love, and serve others as God. We learn to forgive those who have harmed us and to forget and forbear. We learn to be compassionate.

The Ideal Way of Life

Jaṭāyu is a bird. While Rāvaṇa was abducting Sītā and flying away with her, the bird confronted and fought with him. The bird knew very well that it did not have the strength to win the fight, but it thought, "He is doing an adharmic act. If not today, I will die tomorrow. Then, let me die for dharma." And so, he fought with Rāvaṇa. Even a bird in the Rāmāyaṇa considered dharma to be the most essential aspect of life. Dharma should live on. Thus, even a bird shows us the greatness of dharma. We can imbibe many lessons, even from a bird. Jaṭāyu wanted to live for his God, for his dharma. Even death is insignificant in front of his dharma. Jaṭāyu was able to die in the arms of God. He was able to merge with God.

Tyāga — sacrifice or renunciation, is the central message of the Rāmāyaṇa. Many of the characters were willing to renounce everything for the sake of the ideal, their exemplary cause. Rāma, Bharata, Lakṣhmaṇa, Sītā — all of them willingly underwent hardships and pain to fulfill their dharma. Each character outshines the other.

Only a very few people understand the essence of Rāmāyaṇa, its core message. Without imbibing its principles and without awakening devotion within, reading the Rāmāyaṇa has become a mechanical ritual.

We should spend the month of Rāmāyaṇa not only reading the great book, but all the family members should use this opportunity as a platform to sit together and discuss the principles of life and spirituality revealed in it. They should also reflect upon how to live according to those noble ideals. We need to practice those spiritual principles in our lives to gain real benefit from them.

Amma remembers a story: once, there was a debate among scholars in an assembly on which was the best version of the Rāmāyaṇa. One scholar said, "I like one particular narration because it is written in a way that ordinary people can understand." Another scholar said, "I like the Rāmāyaṇa written by a particular person who put it in verse." Many such opinions arose. Another scholar said, "I like my mother's interpretation the best."

"Oh! Did your mother also write an interpretation of the Rāmāyaṇa?" asked the others. The scholar replied, "When I was young, my mother narrated stories from the Rāmāyaṇa to me. I was able to learn many lessons from this — tell the truth, respect elders, have devotion towards God, do not cheat anyone, speak soft words, and many other things. She performed all of her actions by its principles. I think that this is the best version of the Rāmāyaṇa. All her actions were dharmic. She read the Rāmāyaṇa and lived in tune with its principles. Thus, I like the Rāmāyaṇa my mother interpreted for me." We should read the Rāmāyaṇa and live true to its principles. When we teach those values through our own lives, it becomes an accurate model and inspiration for others.

Words are like fire. Fire is a witness to everything. It is light. There is no life without fire. At the same time, if not used with care, it can burn everything to ashes. Words are also like this. Words can take one to the heights of glory, or push one into a deep abyss of degradation. Therefore, each word must be used with great care. Like fire, each word of ours should brighten the lives of others. When we hear another's words, it should inspire us and give us peace. At present, our words do not contain fire; they only give out heat and smoke. They will spread only darkness in the mind of the hearer.

Therefore, we should learn to speak with discernment at all times. We should not react immediately if someone behaves or speaks badly to us. If we see or hear something we do not like, we should not pick a fight or scold the other person at once. There should be a gap between our thoughts and actions. Currently, this gap is not there. Light enters through the gap between thought and action. It is the light of wisdom. In the light of wisdom, we will be able to view and evaluate each situation correctly. And then, we will not respond with words or actions that awaken anger in the other person or cross limits. This is because there is a light within that does not allow us to mistake a snake for a rope or a rope for a snake. We will be able to see the situation as it is. If this awareness dawns within, we will become unable to harbor anger. A seed lying in the hot sun will not germinate. In the light of awareness, the seed of anger will not have the capacity to sprout. We should take care to bring the light of discernment to each thought, word, and deed. We can do so by reading and reflecting on the Rāmāyaṇa. The

Rāmāyaṇa will remove the darkness from and illumine our minds.

A promise Daśharatha gave in a critical situation without proper thought or consideration became the reason for all the sorrow and conflict that ensued. This is why the sages of old prayed, "Let my words be established in my mind, and my mind be established in my words." Both mind and speech should be firmly established in wisdom. Wisdom or discernment is a sign of maturity; it is an inner wealth. Not only should our words and deeds be done with awareness, but each movement should also be meditative.

Many stories in the Itihāsas, the great epics, show how unwise and thoughtless words and deeds have resulted in disastrous consequences. Each example has a lesson for us to learn. By learning from these incidents, we will be able to avoid such circumstances in our lives.

What does Bhīṣhma's story tell us? He made a promise without thinking of its consequences. Because of this, he had to stand by and watch adharma being perpetrated without being able to react.[15] Even when Pāñchālī was being

---

[15] Bhīṣhma made a vow to loyally serve the ruler of the city of Hastināpura. Hastināpura was then ruled

dragged into the assembly and disrobed, Bhīṣhma could only stand by and watch; he could not stop this outrage to a woman's modesty, this act of adharma. His silence was a grave wrong, and he had to pay for it during the last days of his life. He was careful not to break the vow he had made. Bhīṣhma lived in the past, not the present. Our journey will become smooth and benefit society only if we stay in the present as we perform our dharma.

In the Rāmāyaṇa, we see Daśharatha dying heartbroken in the last days of his life, bereft of his son, who had gone into exile to keep his father's words given long ago to his wife. Therefore, we must think twice before we say each and every word. Our words today will determine our life tomorrow. Our life is determined by the words we speak and the actions we take today. The stories in the Rāmāyaṇa and Mahābhārata remind us of the importance of śhraddhā — the focus, awareness, and discernment we need to speak and act.

---

by his adharmic Kaurava grand-nephew Duryōdhana, and this forced him to fight on the side of the Kauravas and adharma during the Mahābhārata war.

A Love that Cannot Be Separated

One of the biggest criticisms against Śhrī Rāma is that he abandoned Sītā. He sent the pregnant Sītā to the forest. Isn't that a grave offense? Ordinary humans like us may be of such an opinion. But we should clearly understand the purity of their love for each other and the oneness of their hearts. There are no questions, no doubts, in selfless love. There is total acceptance. Rāma's decision to leave Sītā Dēvī in the forest was silently accepted by Sītā Dēvī even though Lakṣhmaṇa, his other brothers, Hanumān, and his subjects questioned him within their hearts.

What is the reason for this? In her heart, Sītā knew of Rāma's steadfast love for her; she did not doubt this. Likewise, no force of circumstance had the power to eradicate Sītā from Rāma's heart. Rāma's act is criticized because of the inability to see the depth and strength of their love for each other, because only the outer dimension is seen and evaluated. The ordinary intelligence cannot grasp their supreme and pure love for each other.

What is real love? Real love is when two people totally accept both their virtues and their imperfections, and remain steadfast in love. It is not right to love the rose and abuse the thorns of the rose bush. Sītā never doubted the purity of the love that Rāma had for her. She was well aware that Rāma would never wrong her. Love is not merely physical or emotional. When it is interpreted only in this manner, we are unable to see its subtle and spiritual dimensions.

For a mind established in spirituality, love is a presence. It is an experience that transcends the body, mind, and intellect. This is how we should view the Rāmāyaṇa and the relationship of Sītā and Rāma. In the Rāmāyaṇa, Sītā and Rāma were not two; they were one. When Sītā was sent to the forest, Rāma's heart accompanied her.

Even now, there is a tradition of bringing the seven- or eight-month-old pregnant woman to her parent's home. It is said that from then on, she should remain in the constant remembrance of God, listen to stories from the Purāṇas, and do good deeds. She should always remain happy. The children of those who are sad and upset while they are pregnant are prone to suffer from depression. Amma has seen many such children whose mothers had to undergo suffering while pregnant. Perfect contentment can be experienced only if one really understands the spiritual principles.

Pregnant women should always be happy. Pictures of smiling babies are kept in their rooms so that they remain in a joyous mood. The joy and sorrow of a mother will be reflected in the unborn child.

You must have heard about the stories of Prahlāda[16] and Abhimanyū[17]. Their mothers dozed off while listening to satsang. But even then, tiny sounds could be heard responding to the satsang. Who made those sounds? It was the babies inside their wombs. These are not just stories. Children who have reached their full term in the womb are aware of what is happening around them, they can absorb and retain what they hear and feel. During this time,

---

[16] Son of the demon king Hiraṇyakaśhipu. Prahlāda had unswerving faith in Lord Viṣhṇu who appeared before him in the form of Narasiṁha — the man-lion avatār (incarnation).

[17] The great warrior-son of Arjuna and Subhadra, the sister of Śhrī Kṛiṣhṇa. Arjuna was one of the five Pāṇḍava brothers made famous in the great epic Mahābhārata.

the mothers should be very careful about what they hear and speak.

Sītā's twin children grew within her womb, listening to satsang and to the names of God. Lava and Kuśha were born and went around singing the name of God. They also tied up the horse sent to prove the king's supremacy.[18] Only men of great courage will do so. Finally, it paved the way for them to unite with their father.[19] Understanding the principle behind it is more important than proving the veracity of this story. By pointing fingers and blaming, we have nothing to gain. Many may try to find

---

[18] Reference to the famous aśhvamēdha ritual where in ancient times, a horse was released as part of a fire sacrifice (yajña) performed by a king. The king and his army would follow the horse wherever it went for a year, and would claim all the territory that the horse covered, subduing the local king of that territory if necessary.

[19] In this case it was Rāma who had performed the aśhvamēdha yajña. Lava and Kuśha tying up the horse was an act of defiance. Rāma's brothers went to fight the twins and were defeated by them, which required Rāma to go there himself, resulting in the twins being reunited with their father.

fault, but it will not mar the intrinsic greatness of the Rāmāyaṇa. We will be the losers.

When she became pregnant, Sītā Dēvī desired to stay in gurukulas to meditate and chant mantras. She wanted to immerse herself in remembering God's name and listening to God's stories. Sītā accepted every situation fully, knowing that everything was for the good. Sītā lived in Vālmīki's āśhram, immersing herself in chanting God's names. She gave birth to her twins and brought them up well. Everything turned out for the good. Lava and Kuśha became noble youngsters. Rāma and Sītā were one, bound together by supreme love. Their children also grew up well. There is no Rāma without Sītā and no Sītā without her Rāma. In those days, the kings could marry as many times as they wanted. Rāma did not do so. During the aśhvamēdha yajña, it was essential for the king to be with his wife to perform the rituals. So, Rāma sat beside a golden statue of Sītā and performed the yajña.

The King should always remain a model and an inspiration for his subjects. He should show the ideal way in every situation. There is little meaning in saying, "Rāma abandoned Sītā, Rāma abandoned Lakṣhmaṇa." They were always established in the realm of the Self. They can be compared to a boat floating in the water. But the water should not enter the boat. There is no problem in living in the world. But we should not get entangled in the world. The spider's home is made from the thread it spins from its own body. Rāma and Sītā — and people like them, always reside in the highest state. Even when they interact with the world, they do not develop attachments. Like a snake shedding its skin, they can stay on in the world or leave it. There is nothing for them to reject or to accept. They are established in the brahma-tattva — the supreme, changeless principle that underpins all existence. They come into this world to teach us dharma. They performed their mission to perfection.

Dharmic Values Are Essential

The Rāmāyaṇa helps us to absorb and cement dharmic values and qualities. The characters in the Rāmāyaṇa walked the path of sacrifice, forbearance and service. The Rāmāyaṇa inspires us to emulate such qualities in our life.

Bharata's attitude was, "I am my elder brother's dāsa — his devoted servant." His attitude was, "You are the doer; I am no one." When we drive at night, we see posts lining both sides of the road, painted with reflective paint. The paint illuminates only when the headlights of a car shine on it. It helps us to drive at night without getting into accidents. Suppose a post thinks the cars run due to the light shed by the posts themselves. Actually, it is the reflective paint on the posts that illuminates only when a car's headlights shine on them. Likewise, we forget that we can act only because of the strength God gave us.

Usually, kings wear the crown on their heads. But Bharata bore the pādukās of Śhrī Rāma on his head. He kept the pādukās on the throne and cared for the kingdom with the attitude that Śhrī Rāma was ruling. He lived a life of sacrifice and ruled the kingdom following the dictates of dharma. When Śhrī Rāma returned, Bharata handed over the kingdom to him wholeheartedly.

In earlier days, when some kings traveled, their children would have usurped the throne by the time they returned. Thus, they would lose control over the throne. If they objected, their own children would lock them up in jail. Or they would kill them. We can speak of numerous such incidents. This is where Bharata and Śhrī Rāma become our ideals. The saṁskāra – Bhārat's refined and noble culture, is revealed through them. Śhrī Rāma refused the throne to remain faithful to his father's words and was ready to undergo exile in the forest. Thus, he stands as an exemplar for the entire world. Each character in the Rāmāyaṇa can become an example, a model for us. There is much to learn from them. We should be able to respect and honor our elders. Such a practice will bring discipline into our lives. When we become disciplined, it will help us to stop quarreling and will also awaken the love within. Thus, everyone will become love.

One day, in a gurukula, the guru passed away. Afterwards, no one obeyed anyone. The reason for this was because they had lost their love for each other. They did their jobs as if they were cursed to do so. Earlier, when the guru was alive, millions had come to the āśhram. There was constant mantra japa (repetition) happening and regular satsangs (spiritual discourses) given. After the guru's demise, all these practices became less and less. Observing all this, a disciple became sad, comparing the current state of the āśhram to how it was when the guru was alive: "Everything has been lost. People do not come. Satsangs do not happen. The members have no unity amongst themselves. They are all quarreling."

Hoping to remedy this sorry state, he went to see a siddha[20]. The disciple shared his distress with him: "The āśhram is in a terrible state. No one is going there, and there are no spiritual practices happening as before." The siddha replied, "There is a mahātmā in your āśhram. But no one knows him as he does not reveal his greatness." Before the disciple could ask the

[20] Lit. 'perfected being.' An enlightened or self-realized master.

name of the mahātmā, the siddha went into samādhi.

The disciple was distraught. Who among his brethren could be the mahātmā? How do we find him? He returned with his mind full of thoughts about the identity of the mahātmā: "Who is it? Is it the one who tends the cows? But he doesn't tend them properly. Is it the one who waters the plants? He doesn't water every plant. The mahātmā definitely will not be such a lazy fellow. Is it the one who cooks? He never cooks anything tasty, so it couldn't be him." He thought of each person in the āśhram and found a drawback in each one. Thus, finding fault with everyone, he couldn't find anyone fit to be the mahātmā. He would look at each person and think that he may be the mahātmā, but soon would find a fault in them. One day, he told a brahmachārī friend, "A siddha told me there is a mahātmā here. But before he revealed who he was, the siddha went into samādhi. I cannot identify who this person is." The friend responded, "Let us do one thing. Let us all obey each other. Let us all bow down to each other. Maybe then we will be able to recognize the mahātmā."

Thus, they started prostrating in front of each other. Seeing this, the others in the āśhram also emulated the practice. This custom brought happiness to everyone. They became motivated to do their duties. They started chanting and meditating with faith, focus, and devotion. They had only love for each other. Due to their love for each other, they developed the humility to forgive and forbear. Every one of them developed the same quality. Finally, it is said that all of them attained self-realization. It was the practice of these noble qualities that brought the desired result. When we read the Rāmāyaṇa, we should also awaken the noble qualities mentioned in it. We should inculcate the dharma of the Rāmāyaṇa into our own lives.

The Rāmāyaṇa helps us build a family life based on love, unity, and mutual respect. It is a fertile field of devotion towards the father, mother, husband, wife, and love for the guru. It showcases the love of brothers for each other, ideal friendships, and other good qualities.

In earlier days, people entered the householder's life only after attending the gurukulas and finishing their education there. They knew the ultimate goal of life. For the husband and wife, family life was a way to attain this goal. They were also content to live with what they had and to help each other. Nowadays, the gurukula system of education does not exist, so values have also deteriorated. Each person has their own likes. Their only goal is their own pleasure. If they are thwarted, they will separate and live by themselves.

Amma remembers a story: an eighty-five-year-old wife and her ninety-year-old husband went to the temple. They had been married for sixty years. Standing in front of the idol they both prayed. The husband prayed, "O Lord, let us both live until I am one hundred years old. Please make this desire come true." Hearing this, the wife prayed, "O Lord! Please bless me to live one year longer than that."

Listening to his wife's prayer, the husband burst out in fury and started shouting at his wife. "Usually, sumaṅgalī women[21] pray to die while their husbands are still alive. Why did you pray like this? I understand the motive behind your prayer. After my death, you wish to live with someone else. I always had the doubt that

---

[21] Sumaṅgalī refers to a 'woman whose husband is still alive.'

you loved someone else. Now I am certain." The wife asked, "Why are you accusing me of that? I prayed like this because I want to live in heaven."

The husband countered, "Don't we go to heaven when we die together?" The wife replied, "Life with you has been one constant quarrel. I have not had a single moment of peace. You are fighting with me even now in front of the temple. You are always angry with me and insulting me. Life with you is hell. If I were to live one year longer than you, I would have one year of peace. That would be my heaven."

The Rāmāyaṇa shows us how to lead a family life, the ideal relationship between brothers, the behaviors we should avoid in our lives, etc.

Rāma and Sītā exemplify the ideal relationship between husband and wife. Now, many find fault with Rāma, saying that he abandoned Sītā in the forest. Rāma can never abandon Sītā. Sītā could never even dream of another man in Rāma's place. She knew that as well as being her husband, Rāma was also the King of Ayōdhyā. For a king, the kingdom is more important than the family. The king is answerable to his subjects, more so than to his wife.

A military officer came home on leave. The very next day, he received a message to report back to duty; there was a conflict at the border. After a long time, he had been given leave to spend some time with his family. A responsible military officer will not say, "I have not been able to spend even two days with my wife and children. Hence, I will not go back now." He will immediately return to active duty. Even if she is sad, the wife will allow her husband to leave. Thus, our duty to our country is above our duty to our family.

For Rāma, his country took precedence over everything else. His country and his subjects' interests were foremost in his mind when he sent Sītā to the forest. Sītā was pregnant and longing to stay in a spiritual atmosphere. When children lie in their mother's womb, they should listen to the names of God. They should also grow up listening to sacred chants and hymns exalting the divine. Through his decision, Rāma was able to give Sītā such an environment. By sending Sītā to the forest, he also put an end to the doubts in the minds of his subjects.

Rāma went through great hardship to bring Sītā back, whom Rāvaṇa had kidnapped. No one talks about this aspect of Rāma.

No one remembers the Rāma who went around like a madman calling out, "Sītā... Sītā," pleading and demanding that the trees and vines, the birds and animals, give him the whereabouts of his Sītā. If their wives were lost, how many husbands would be ready to regain them, braving the hardship and obstacles faced by Rāma? Rāma could never see another woman in Sītā's place.

Earlier, a king could marry as many times as he wanted. Rāma's father, Daśharatha, had three wives. But Rāma stood firm in his vow to have only one consort. Śhrī Rāma took birth and lived as a human being, showing us through his own life how to live a life established in dharma.

As a husband, he should take care of his family's affairs. As a king, he should rule the country, see to the welfare of his subjects, and live a life true to dharma without swerving even in the least. When we move forward firmly established in dharma, it may not be possible to satisfy everyone. When traveling on the path of dharma, severe decisions must sometimes be made. When responsibilities are performed with an emphasis on dharma, we may have to give up some things in life. This is what Rāma shows us with his own life.

We should not see Rāma and Sītā merely on a superficial level. Sītā is said to be the symbol of the mind. Whatever is made of the five great elements comes into being, exists, and then returns back to earth. Sītā was discovered in a furrow in a field emerging from the earth. She returned to the earth as it split asunder to accept her. Her ātman merged in Rāma. After our death, our bodies will merge into the earth. If we live in Rāma's remembrance, our ātman will merge with Rāma. We should remember this spiritual principle.

Sanātana Dharma is like mathematics. We will get the correct answer only if we do the calculations correctly.

Some people say that Lakṣhmaṇa's actions towards Śhūrpaṇakhā[22] were not right. It was

---

[22] A demoness and sister of Rāvaṇa. She took the form of a beautiful woman to entice first Rāma and then Lakṣhmaṇa. When rejected by both, she tried to attack Sītā, causing Lakṣhmaṇa to stop her by cutting off her nose.

lust that made Śhūrpaṇakhā approach Rāma and Lakṣhmaṇa. Both of them were married. During their years of forest exile, they were observing many vows. Both of them were living the lives of ascetics. They could never accept Śhūrpaṇakhā. Even though they tried very hard to explain this to her, Śhūrpaṇakhā, blinded by lust, could not accept it. If someone serves us a dish we are allergic to, we will say no. If he insists, we will also be more assertive in our refusal. We will stop him from serving it with our own hands if he still tries to serve it to us. We may also get angry. We will not eat it, even when thinking we do not want to hurt the feelings of the person serving us.

Rāma and Lakṣhmaṇa were not prepared to swerve even an inch from their vows. But Śhūrpaṇakhā refused to listen to their words. When a lion closes in for the kill, we will face it with whatever weapons we have. If we show compassion towards the lion, our lives will be endangered.

Śhūrpaṇakhā is the symbol of lust. When circumstances arise in which lust attacks the mind, there should be no consideration for it. This is the principle that we should imbibe from this story. If we bow down our heads before kāma (lust) it will swallow us up. Before that, we need to cut off its nose. The need for constant vigilance is what we should learn from this incident.

There Is No "I" in Dharmic Thinking

The Rāmāyaṇa teaches us about the importance of dharma in our lives. We should build our lives on the foundation of dharma. Only then will we gain the strength to overcome challenges and move forward. If we abandon dharma, even a minor incident can sap our energy.

Our worth is decided not just by the wealth we amass, the positions we hold, or how many people have honored and adored us. Many billionaires and rulers who came before us have returned to merge with the earth. Among them, how many do we still remember? Yet, even if they have not been very successful in worldly terms, those who have stood firm in their values still hold a place in our hearts even after their death.

The lives of those who, like candles, burn themselves out to give light to others will continue to light the path for thousands, even after their death. The lives of the devotees of God are ample proof. In their lives, God holds the highest place, more than anything else. They can never harm anyone, as love for God brims over in their hearts. They can never travel outside the path of dharma, as they follow God's path.

Prahlāda is honored by this world because he defied his adharmic father and sought refuge in God. Vibhīṣhaṇa is accepted by this world more than Kumbhakarṇa[23] because he did not ally himself to adharma in the name of indebtedness to Rāvaṇa; he saw dharma and dedication to God as supreme and sought refuge in Rāma. The world worships Śhrī Buddha only because he gave up his kingdom and the throne and saw that his highest dharma was to seek the Self. The world will always remember, honor, and worship great souls. Power, name, fame, and wealth do not last. They will come today and leave tomorrow. They are like imitation gold. Their sheen and glitter are temporary. Therefore, we must make a firm resolve to walk on the path of truth.

Only God's face is the truth — all else is a mask. Life will attain perfection only when we see God's eternal face everywhere and in everything. Those who wish to realize God or

---

[23] Both Vibhīṣhaṇa and Kumbhakarṇa were Rāvaṇa's brothers.

attain the highest dharma of liberation should carefully study life's circumstances while performing their intrinsic dharma. We should closely observe the mind. While performing our svadharma, our intrinsic duties and responsibilities, our attitude should be that of someone enacting their part in a drama.

A person acting in a drama has set dialogues for different situations. There are expressions of face and voice that they must use right at the moment they are needed. If the actors mistime their expressions and dialogues, if they are a bit late or a bit early, the audience will not react as expected. When an actor raises his hand to slap another on the cheek, others on stage will be expected to stop him. If they do not stop him at the exact moment, the slap will land on the other actor's cheek. This may be inappropriate for the scene.

Similarly, what would it be like if an actor says he will only say his lines and then exit the scene without listening and responding to his fellow actors? The drama will not become a success if all the actors and actresses do not cooperate with and work in harmony with each other. People will jeer at the play and throw stones. Sometimes, the drama company may have to close down. When a musical concert is being held, many instruments are played, like violins, flutes, etc. Each musician should concentrate on their part. The harmony will be lost if even one instrument goes off-key. Even if someone sings beautifully, the rhythm will be lost if there is some mistake in the background music. The music will become a cacophony.

Likewise, each of us has a part to play in the drama of life. We should also consider the characters and situations around us when we play our part. We should align ourselves with them. Otherwise, not only will this drama of life fall apart, but each one of the characters will have to grieve. Dharma is the rhythm, the melody, and the harmony that binds together each character in this drama of life, including nature. We should be able to tune ourselves to and obey this rhythm, and become an ideal and inspiration for others. The Rāmāyaṇa trains and motivates us to be such human beings.

Dharma is eternal — it transcends time and space. The concepts of love and peace are common to every country. Their nature remains the same from country to country. Likewise, dharma is the same everywhere. Sanātana Dharma is also the same everywhere. Harmony is possible in every situation when we obey the intrinsic dharma relevant to it. Love and compassion towards fellow beings is a dharma that should be observed at all times and in all places. Yet, there are also duties and responsibilities particular to the time and place.

There are specific rules to be observed when we drive a vehicle on the road. The driver's dharma is to obey the rules. Accidents happen when we do not obey the rules. There are designated areas in airports for smokers. They are allowed to smoke only in that area. If we defy this and smoke in public areas, it creates uneasiness and discomfort for others. It is not dharma. We must obey our intrinsic dharma to maintain the harmony of the family, society, and the universe.

Nowadays, people leave dharma behind as their only aim is selfish gain. This is the reason why there are so many problems besetting the family and society now. Marital bonds break up over trivial issues. The children are bereft and left to themselves. Many children come to Amma and ask, "Amma, will I ever be able, in this birth, to sit on the laps of my mother and father like other children?" Amma watches their eyes well up with tears. Their sorrow is embedded deep in their hearts and may later become depression. We have abandoned dharma, which is why we face many problems today. Grace should bless us to bring about a positive change. The entrenched notion of "I" — the ego, is the leading cause of society's degradation. It can be overcome by practicing our dharma.

Amma remembers a story: once, there was a racehorse which always came first in every race it ran. In that land, there was a very wealthy man who was also a troublemaker. The man who owned the racehorse became famous all over the country because his horse always won. The man's fame also spread to neighboring countries. The wealthy man became very jealous of the man's popularity and wanted to own that horse by hook or by crook. He asked the horse's owner to sell it to him, offering him as much money as he might ask for. The owner loved the horse like his son and was not willing to sell it. The wealthy man cajoled and pressured him but to no avail. Finally, he threatened the man and took his horse away by force.

The owner had trained the horse in a particular way. Therefore, this racehorse was very different from other horses. When you sit on the saddle and say "I," the horse will run. When you say, "God!" the horse will stop. The rich man was ignorant of this. A huge crowd gathered in front of his home, hoping for a glimpse of the famous horse. When he saw the crowd, the rich man's ego became inflated sky-high. He straddled the horse, held the reins, and asked the crowd, "Do you want to see how I ride this horse?"

When it heard the sound "I," the horse broke into a fast gallop. The crowd ran behind, enjoying the speed of the horse. After a while, the man tried to stop the horse by pulling on the reins. But as the horse was trained in that particular way, it did not stop running. The man tried many different ways to stop the horse, but it continued galloping up a hill. Suddenly, he saw a deep canyon appear before him. The horse was running right towards it. Try as he might, the arrogant man could not stop the horse nor change its course. By then, the horse had reached the clifftop. In front was a canyon dropping down hundreds of feet below. If the horse fell into it, neither the man nor the horse would survive. As all doors closed before him, the rich man looked up and said, "O God!" The horse suddenly braked and came to a stop. They had escaped from great danger by a mere hair's breadth.

By then, those running behind the horse admiring its speed, approached. They started praising the dextrous skill of the rich man, who had stopped the horse at the very last minute. Hearing this, the man's ego and arrogance reinflated. He said haughtily, "Did you see how I stopped the horse?" As soon as the horse heard the word "I," it leapt into the canyon. Neither the horse nor the rich man could ever be found again, as they had fallen into the depths of the canyon. Likewise, the sense of 'I' in us is the cause of our destruction. If we are able to remove the sense of 'I' and realize that we are 'God's servants,' then God will save us from all danger. Or, if obstacles come our way, he will give us the strength to endure and overcome them.

If all four people in a home desire to be kings, there will only be war. In the Rāmāyaṇa, no one desired to be king. The four brothers were willing to sacrifice anything for the other three. They found joy in the other's gain. Each character's life in the Rāmāyaṇa is a lesson for us to learn from. If we are able to absorb these lessons, it will lead us to liberation.

Amma remembers an incident that happened in Seattle: a running race was being held for children who were mentally challenged. During the race, one of the participants fell. Another child saw this, stopped running, turned around, and went to help the fallen child stand up again. Seeing this, all the other contestants came running to help up the fallen child. Then, holding hands together, they started running towards the finish line. It became a race in which all the participants took the first prize. The compassion within them made every child a winner. Everyone was given a prize. Compassion is needed to gain real victory in life. We can also see this in the Rāmāyaṇa.

The Rāmāyaṇa teaches us not just to love humankind but also nature and all the flora and fauna of nature. When we read the Rāmāyaṇa, we can experience the divine consciousness that pulsates in every single atom of every being.

The Rāmāyaṇa teaches us to perform sacrifices for the sake of the country and society. Rāma, Bharata, Sītā, and Hanumān are our models in this regard.

Rāmāyaṇa Makes Relationships Strong

In olden times, the month of Karkidaka was said to be one of poverty. In those days, government servants holding secure jobs and having steady income were very few. During this month, there would be no demand for laborers, and other jobs were also not available. It was a month of heavy rains and floods. Most of the population would face poverty.

It is the month when people hold on tightly to God to reduce their hardship. It is the time when we pray devoutly to God to save and protect everyone. God was the only refuge for the ordinary human being. Therefore, one needs to have an attitude of surrender towards God. The Rāmāyaṇa is read to reduce the hardships and damages that happen during this month of Karkidaka rains. The Rāmāyaṇa helps reduce the pain of poverty and resolves family and individual problems.

When you read the Rāmāyaṇa, the varied situations described in the stories will give strength to the mind. Within the family, the

Rāmāyaṇa has greatly helped us develop respect and obedience to the words of experienced elders and love between siblings. When problems arise in the family, the elders take similar situations in the Rāmāyaṇa as precedent and try to solve the present problem. The Rāmāyaṇa shows us the ideal way to lead a family life.

Many people read the Rāmāyaṇa to increase their puṇya or karmic merits, and decrease their pāpa or karmic demerits. But the ideal way to peruse the Rāmāyaṇa is to gain pure devotion and love for God. We must read the Rāmāyaṇa, knowing the spiritual principles behind it, to increase our devotion and to have complete surrender. The Rāmāyaṇa should become a spiritual sadhana for listening, reflecting, and meditating.

Some say that the Rāmāyaṇa is only a literary composition, and that the characters are fictional. Is there any other composition like the Rāmāyaṇa that has touched the hearts and lives of millions of people in countries all over the world? It has become a part of their culture and their worship. Other than the Rāmāyaṇa, no one can show any other work of literature that has positively impacted the lives of millions.

Only the histories of people who once lived can greatly influence the world.

Amma has seen eighty to eighty-five-year-old mothers and fathers in many families. Like in the Rāmāyaṇa, they are all of one mind in thinking that they should not give any sorrow to their elder brother or trouble their younger brother. Many of them have strong bonds with their siblings. But we do not see this characteristic in their grandchildren. On the contrary, a few among them have no qualms in hurting even their own parents. The parents would come to Amma and cry about the difficult situations their children put them in.

In joint families, if the father dies, the elder brother takes care of the family. They love their younger brothers and their children like their own. Even if they neglect their needs, they will ensure others have everything they need. Amma knows many such joint families. In earlier days, because they had read and understood the Rāmāyaṇa, we could see the characters of Bharata and Lakṣhmaṇa among brothers in many families. But today's children do not know those principles and noble values, as no one has told them. We can see the ill effects in society arising from the lack of this knowledge. Many people are led by cruel thoughts to become wealthy, even by betraying or killing others.

Two brothers lived in neighboring houses. The younger one had no children. The elder thought, "Oh! My brother has no children to care for him in his old age. It would be good to give him some of our wealth." The elder brother called his wife, and they started filling sacks of rice, and taking and storing them in the younger brother's house at night without anyone noticing. At the same time, the younger brother thought, "I have no children, whereas my brother has his own. What need do I have for all this wealth?" So, the younger brother started filling sacks of rice and transported them stealthily at night to his brother's home. His wife helped him. One day, the elder brother's sons saw his father taking sacks of rice over to his younger brother. They said, "Father, why are you doing this? Why do you take everything from here to there? He has no children. Let us put on a show of love and get him to sign all his wealth over to us without delay."

This is the advice given by today's children. Today, some will not hesitate to poison the younger brother after getting him to sign all his wealth over to them. This is the difference between the present generation and previous generations. Then, there was a strong bond of love between siblings. Now, all this is disappearing. The reason is that we have lost our value system.

When we read the Rāmāyaṇa, we should be aware of the essence of spirituality and live in dharma, faithful to our rights and responsibilities. Only then will we get the real benefit of the Rāmāyaṇa.

Observing Vows Is Good for Our Health

When the rainy season starts, one becomes sick more often. Many deaths happen in the month of Karkidaka. When Amma was younger, she heard grandmothers say that they would know how many grandchildren they have only after the tenth day of the month of Karkidaka. The lack of sunlight and the cold also adversely affects the human mind. In such a situation, the Rāmāyaṇa is an ideal tool to restore energy and self-confidence in our lives. We read the Rāmāyaṇa to become Rāma. We read the Bhāgavatam to become Kṛiṣhṇa. This means that we have to incorporate into our lives the life lessons they have taught us. Thus, we should bring about a transformation in our lives. Thus, we should also rise to perfection like them.

In the month of Karkidaka, we are unable to digest food properly because of the increased cold and the moist climate. This is why many people observe fasting vows in Karkidaka. They will eat very little food and often eat only once a day, so the body will digest well. We must eat food that maintains our health and makes us stronger and able to resist disease. Good food habits are coming into vogue, like the Karkidaka Kañji, a special recipe of rice gruel with medicinal spices.

During this month, meat will be digested slowly and may cause new diseases. For the sake of our health, it is better to take light food in smaller quantities. During this time, we should read the Rāmāyaṇa and bring to mind good thoughts that help us to live established in the spiritual principles and awaken awareness of the Self. Thus, by reinvigorating ourselves, the mind will become healthy. Making the mind happy and energetic is like the sun dawning within. So, we must imbibe the spiritual principles and live according to them. We should take care not to let go of dharmic thoughts.

It has been found that during the days of religious festivals, the number of sick people is reduced by thirty per cent. We can confirm this truth by checking with the hospitals. This is because the mind becomes enthusiastic, energetic, and joyful during the festival season. Also, because many vows are observed at this time, it keeps a lot of diseases at bay. The number of patients admitted to hospitals will reduce considerably on these days.

During the Sabarimala pilgrimage season[24] and other temple festival seasons, the mind and body become healthy and filled with enthusiasm, energy, and joy as alcohol and meat are not consumed, and the focus is on chanting God's names and observing vows. This might be the reason why the hospitals report fewer patients being admitted during these times.

There was a time when the Rāmāyaṇa was read during the month of Karkidaka, and people lived in harmony with the spiritual principles espoused in the book. Long ago, grandmothers would read the Rāmāyaṇa, and the grandchildren listening to it would live by its spiritual principles. There was respect and obedience towards elders.

In this part of Kerala, fishermen going to sea will tie a piece of cloth around their heads

---

[24] Sabarimala is a famous temple in Kerala dedicated to Lord Ayyappa. Before the pilgrimage to the temple, hundreds of thousands of male devotees participate each year in the 41-day vows, during which they maintain celibacy, follow a vegetarian diet, and practice austerity and discipline.

to avoid the sun's heat. Like those who wish to grow mustaches like their elders, the young boys would also go around with a piece of cloth tied around their heads. But, if they saw older people around, they would immediately untie the cloth from their heads. Likewise, if they saw their father, elder brothers, or uncles; the sons, younger brothers, and nephews would respectfully untie the cloth from around their heads.

They did so as a mark of humility. When older people entered the house, the younger ones would humbly stand up. The mother would stand up when the father came home, and the father would stand up when the grandmother entered the house. Seeing this, the children would also emulate them. All these good and virtuous habits are now lost. Nowadays, things have come to such a pass that the parents have to stand up when their son comes home. Children learn by seeing the habits of their elders. Now, there is no one to model this good behavior for them.

Do Not Prejudge

Our reading of the Rāmāyaṇa can be compared to an elephant taking a bath. After bathing, the elephant throws dirt all over its body again. Our reading of the Rāmāyaṇa should not be like this. We read spiritual books, but if we do not live according to the values they espouse, we slide back into wrongdoing. There is no use in reading spiritual books without imbibing the spiritual principles revealed through them. It is like putting a heap of sugar on one side and ants on the other side. The ants will at once eat up the sugar we deposit.

We should sincerely strive to adopt noble values in our lives. Only if we live those values does praying and reading the Rāmāyaṇa become meaningful. We will receive the results both within and in the external world.

The Rāmāyaṇa is the vehicle of our culture; it is not merely a book of moral advice. When we read and listen to the Rāmāyaṇa, when we taste its sweetness, unknowingly, a noble culture becomes embedded within us. It will purify us. The Rāmāyaṇa has the strength to do so. We will be able to know right from wrong and act accordingly. We will try very hard to harness our minds. When we read the Rāmāyaṇa in-depth, we will be able to absorb its values. We read the Rāmāyaṇa to become Rāma. If so, we will observe and read about all the characters of the Rāmāyaṇa. We will try to imbibe their goodness and try to act upon it. We will gain the strength to do so. We can savor the Rāmāyaṇa's sweetness when we read it without any prejudgements.

A mother saw her son holding an apple in each hand. She asked him, "Son, will you give me an apple?" At once, the child bit into one of the apples. His mother felt upset at the seeming selfishness of the child but asked again, "Give me an apple, child." At once, the child bit into the other apple. The mother felt angry and disappointed. This was not how she had brought up her son. She felt like hitting him and scolding him. She caught hold of her son's hand, intending to slap him. She also tried to grab an apple from him. Then the child said, "No mother, the other apple is sweeter. I shall give you the other one."

The child had bitten into the apple to find out which one was sweeter. When he bit into the first one, he found it to be very sour. When he bit into the second one, he found it to be sweet. The angry mother tried to grab the sour apple. Then the child said with innocence, "No mother, the other one is sweeter." The mother had prejudged his actions and started to scold and even to beat the child. We are unable to open our hearts or understand others if we look at them with preconceived notions. Our hearts are closed due to prejudgements. So, we should approach the Rāmāyaṇa without prejudice. Then, we will be able to accept the Rāmāyaṇa wholeheartedly.

May Amma's children learn to accept the Rāmāyaṇa without prejudgements and with an open heart, patiently understanding each character and situation.

Vālmīki Rāmāyaṇa

Sage Vālmīki composed the Rāmāyaṇa. Sages are people who have deep insight into human life. Through their compositions, we will also gain that insight.

The life of Sage Vālmīki is inextricably linked to the name of Rāma. The meaning of the word Rāma is the supreme truth, brahman — the absolute. Rāma is that in which the yōgis find bliss. Some words have an inherent strength. Rāma is such a word. It brings ashore the jīva or individual soul, trapped in the sorrows of saṁsāra — the relentless cycle of death and rebirth. Even if the Rāmāyaṇa fades away from this world, the strength of Rāma's name will never lose its power.

There is a story regarding Rāma's name and Vālmīki's birth: once, a brahmin's cow died due to his negligence. To gain release from the demerits of this action, he went to the āśhram of a sage, but the sage was not there. The sage's disciple advised him to chant the name of Rāma out loud four times. This would absolve him of all sin. The brahmin did so.

After a while, the sage returned. Hearing what happened, the guru became angry with his disciple, "Chanting the name of Rāma even once will clear every difficulty. Asking the brahmin to chant the name of Rāma four times shows your lack of trust. Therefore, as atonement, may you live an entire life chanting the name of Rāma." This disciple was later reborn as Vālmīki.

This story emphasizes the importance of faith. More important than the number of God's names that we chant, or the spiritual practices we perform, is faith. More important is the strength of our faith and our one-pointed focus. If our faith is firm and strong, traditions and practices are not important. Self-realization is possible in an instant.

Another story comes to mind: a brahmin had a wayward son. The brahmin advised and scolded him often to wean him away from his bad habits. Nothing had any effect. Finally, the brahmin went to a mahātmā and confided in him about his son's bad habits. The mahātmā blessed him by asking him to worship the Lord by offering berries from the bael tree to the sacred fire. Then, his son would relinquish his bad habits.

The brahmin took a vow and offered bael berries to the fire. This went on for weeks and months. He neither had a vision of the Lord nor did his son reform. The brahmin had a servant. Seeing his master spending sleepless nights, and becoming frail by eating very little food, the servant became very distressed. One day, he asked the brahmin, "Why have you been performing this ritual sacrifice for such a long time?"

The brahmin replied, "If this yajña is successful, Agnidēva, the god of fire, will appear before me, and my son will become good. I will continue this yajña until the fire god appears. Hearing this, the servant said that if his master allowed it, he would offer the bael berries to the fire just one time. The brahmin said, "Don't talk foolishness. You have not taken any vows, nor do you have any disciplined spiritual practice. How will you succeed if you offer the berries to the fire?" The servant said, "It may be so, but allow me to offer oblations to the fire just once." The brahmin agreed.

The servant took the bael berries in his hand, saw the Lord within his heart and prayed, "Lord, please bless me with this one berry that I offer." With this prayer, he offered the berry to the flame, and Agnidēva appeared. The brahmin saw this and asked the god of fire, "O Lord, I have worshiped you for a long time doing great spiritual austerities, but you did not bless me. However, you were instantly pleased by the ritual sacrifice offered by this person who has no scriptural knowledge, nor does he perform any spiritual austerities." Agnidēva replied, "You were disciplined in your austerities. Still, you did not have firm faith; your attitude was selfish. You did not surrender to me. But he had both firm faith and surrender. He also made a strong resolve." Saying this, Agnidēva disappeared. After a few days, the brahmin's son reformed and became a good human being. The fruits of our actions will be swift and sure where there is firm faith and a strong resolve (saṅkalpa).

The Rāmāyaṇa is not entirely the story of a few individuals or kings. It is not entirely the story of human beings. The characters in the Rāmāyaṇa include humans, birds, animals, trees, mountains, rivers, the ocean, and indeed, all of nature. Each one has stories to tell us of the greatness of dharma, sacrifice, and selflessness. The Rāmāyaṇa is a story of love, unity, and fidelity to the highest ideals. This is the greatness and sweetness of the Rāmāyaṇa.

The observance of the Rāmāyaṇa month and reading of the Rāmāyaṇa is slowly disappearing from our homes. This will be a terrible loss to society. The blessings showered upon us by the Rāmāyaṇa impact every layer of human existence. All those who love our saṁskāra — our noble and ancient cultural heritage, and values — should cherish the Rāmāyaṇa as a priceless treasure in our hearts and homes.

To appreciate pure language and literature, we should read the Vālmīki Rāmāyaṇa. To understand the profound relationship between humans, nature, and all living beings, we should read the Vālmīki Rāmāyaṇa. To immerse ourselves in nature's beauty, we should read the Vālmīki Rāmāyaṇa. If we desire to live true to the highest ideals and dharmic values, we should understand the Vālmīki Rāmāyaṇa. If we need to know about a human love with no caste or creed, we should understand the Vālmīki Rāmāyaṇa. If we need to know the history of the life of a mahātmā who threw away, like a piece of straw, all his life's joys and comforts for the sake of his subjects' good and welfare, we should understand the Vālmīki Rāmāyaṇa.

The Rāmāyaṇa is pure sweetness. It is pure auspiciousness. It is a sweet fruit of pure medicinal goodness without even an outer skin that needs to be peeled away. Let the fellowship of human beings enjoy this sweet fruit for centuries to come. Let them exult in its beauty and goodness and thus become pure-hearted. Let grace bless everyone to achieve this.

Glossary

Abhimanyū: the great warrior-son of Pāṇḍava prince Arjuna and Subhadra (sister of Śhrī Kṛiṣhṇa).

āchārya: one who consolidates the essentials of the scriptures, establishes them in tradition, and observes them in practice.

adharma: unrighteousness; deviation from natural harmony.

adharmic: unrighteous.

Adhyātma Rāmāyaṇa: a spiritual rendering of the traditional *Vālmīki Rāmāyaṇa* in Sanskrit, usually attributed to sage Vyāsa.

Agnidēva: the god of fire. One of the most important deities in the *Vēdic* tradition.

aiśhvarya: auspicious prosperity, worldly progress.

amma: Malayalam word for 'mother.'

Aṅgada: a strong and valiant *Vānara*, son of Vāli, who was sent by Rāma as ambassador to persuade Rāvaṇa to return Sītā.

Añjanā: mother of Hanumān.

annadāna: gift or offering of food.

ārādhanā: adoration of the divine.

Arjuna: great archer and one of the heroes of the *Mahābhārata*. It is Arjuna whom Kṛiṣhṇa addresses in the *Bhagavad Gītā*.

artha: goal; wealth; substance. One of the four *puruṣhārthas* (goals of human endeavor).

aśhōkavana: the forest grove where Sītā was held captive by Rāvaṇa.

āśhram: 'place of striving.' A place where spiritual seekers and aspirants live or visit, in order to lead a spiritual life. It is usually the home of a spiritual master, saint or ascetic, who guides the aspirants.

aśhvamēdha: a famous ritual where in ancient times, a horse was released as part of a fire sacrifice performed by a king. The king and his army would follow the horse wherever it went for a year, and would claim all the territory that the horse covered.

asuric: demonic.

ātmā (ātman): the true self. The essential nature of our real existence. One of the fundamental tenets of *Sanātana Dharma* is that we are not the physical body, feelings, mind, intellect, or personality. We are the eternal, pure, unblemished self.

avatār: from Sanskrit root 'ava-tarati' — 'to come down.' Divine incarnation.

avatārapuruṣha: incarnation of God in human form.

ayana: journey.

Ayōdhyā: ancient city; birthplace and kingdom of Lord Rāma.

Āyurvēda: traditional Indian system of medicine.

Āyurvēdic: pertaining to Āyurvēda.

Ayyappa: god of truth and righteousness, the deity of Sabarimala temple in Kerala, the son of goddess Mōhinī (incarnation of Lord Viṣhṇu) and Lord Śhiva.

bael tree: *Aegle mermelos,* sacred tree that is used in Āyurvēda for its medicinal properties. It is called *kūvaḷam* in Malayalam and also known as the bilva tree sacred to Lord Śhiva.

bhaga: the six blessed qualities, viz. *jñāna* (knowledge), *aiśhvarya* (sovereignty), śhakti (energy), *bala* (might), *vīrya* (valor) and *tējas* (spiritual splendor). One who has all these qualities is known as *bhagavān* (God) or *bhagavatī* (Goddess).

Bhagavad Gītā: 'Song of the Lord,' it consists of eighteen chapters of verses in which Lord Kṛiṣhṇa advises Arjuna. The advice is given on the battlefield of Kurukṣhētra, just before the righteous Pāṇḍavas fight the unrighteous Kauravas. It is a practical guide to overcoming crises in one's personal or social life and is the essence of *Vēdic* wisdom.

Bhāgavata Purāṇa: also known as *Bhāgavatam*. One of the eighteen *Purāṇas*, a devotional Sanskrit composition narrating the life, pastimes, and teachings of various incarnations of Viṣhṇu, chiefly that of Lord Kṛiṣhṇa.

bhakti: devotion for God.

Bhārat: India.

Bharata: the son of Daśharatha and Kaikēyī who ruled the kingdom of Āyōdhyā for the fourteen years of his eldest brother Rāma's absence. He is particularly known for his willingness to forgo power and comfort out of pure love and loyalty towards Rāma, and for the sake of upholding *dharma* and selflessly serving the people.

Bhāratīya: pertaining to Bhārat; Indian.

Bhīṣhma: patriarch of the Pāṇḍava and Kaurava clans. Though he fought on the side of the Kauravas during the *Mahābhārata* War, he championed dharma and was sympathetic to the righteous Pāṇḍavas.

Bhōja (king): 11th century Indian king from the Paramāra dynasty known for both his military prowess and his intellectual pursuits.

brahma-tattva: the supreme, changeless principle that underpins all existence.

brahmachārī: celibate male disciple who practices spiritual disciplines under a guru's guidance; '*brahmachāriṇī*' is the female equivalent.

brahman: the absolute reality, supreme being; the whole; that which encompasses and pervades everything, and is one and indivisible.

brahmin: also known as *brāhmaṇa*, a member of the priestly caste whose duty it is to study and teach the *Vēdas*.

Buddha: from 'budh,' meaning 'to wake up;' also, a reference to sage Gautama Buddha, a spiritual master whose teachings form the foundation of Buddhism.

Chārvāka: the materialists of ancient India, a school of philosophy that regards sensory experience alone as a valid source of knowledge.

chirañjīvī: one of the 'immortals' who remain embodied on earth until the end of the present *kalpa*, the present cycle of creation, preservation, and destruction of the universe. Depending on the source, seven to nine individuals are mentioned to belong to this class of being.

dakṣhiṇa: an offering or gift, usually in the form of money.

dāsa: devoted servant or follower.

Daśharatha: father of Rāma and King of Kōśhala.

dēva: deity or god; divine being; celestial being. *Dēva* is the masculine form. The feminine equivalent is *dēvī*.

Dēvī: goddess; Divine Mother.

dharma: 'that which upholds (creation).' Generally refers to the harmony of the universe; a righteous code of conduct; sacred duty; or the eternal law.

dharmapatnī: wife who fulfills her duties and obligations according to *dharma.*

dharmic: in accordance with *dharma.*

Duryōdhana: eldest son of Dhṛitarāṣhṭra, rival of the Pāṇdavas and chief antagonist in the *Mahabhārata* epic, often cited as an example of the harmful effects of unrestrained ambition, jealousy, and pride.

Ezhuthachan: Thunchaththu Ezhuthachan was great 16th century poet, considered as the Father of Malayalam Literature.

gandharvas: a class of celestial beings who are musicians, singers, and dancers who entertain the *dēvas* or gods in heaven.

Garuḍa: deity in the form of an eagle who is Lord Viṣhṇu's vehicle and regarded as the king of all birds.

Gītā: lit. 'song'. Often used to refer to the *Bhagavad Gītā.*

guru: spiritual teacher.

gurukula: lit. 'guru's family.' The home or āśhram of a guru where children go to live and study under the guru's guidance.

Hanumān: the *Vānara* disciple and companion of Rāma and one of the key characters in the *Rāmāyaṇa.*

Hastināpura: capital city of the Kuru Kingdom, prominently featured in the *Mahābhārata.*

Hindu: follower of Hinduism, the religion native to India that is also called Sanātana Dharma.

Hiraṇyakaśhipu: powerful demon king and father of Prahlāda who was slain by Narasiṁha, the man-lion incarnation of Lord Viṣhṇu.

Indrajit: son of Rāvaṇa.

indriya: sense, sende organ.

Itihāsas: the two great epics *Rāmāyaṇa* and *Mahābhārata.*

japa: repeated chanting of a *mantra.*

Jaṭāyu: the vulture who valiantly fought Rāvaṇa in an attempt to rescue Sītā.

jitēndriya: 'someone who has conquered his senses' — composed of 'jit' meaning 'conquered' or 'subdued', and 'indriya' meaning 'senses' or 'sense organs.' *Jitēndra* is a variant spelling that is a popular first name.

jīvātmā: individual soul or self. Sometimes referred to as just '*jīva*.'

jñāna: knowledge of the truth. A *jñānī* is one who knows the truth.

jñānadāna: gift or offering of knowledge in form of spiritual teaching or reading from sacred scripture.

Kaikēyī: second wife of Daśharatha and mother of Bharata.

Kaiyyōnni: *Eclipta alba*, a medicinal herb also known as 'false daisy.'

Kākabhuśhuṇḍi: name of the crow that advised Garuḍa in a sub-story contained in the Uttar Kāṇḍ of *Rāmcharitmānas*.

kāma: lust, or desire in general.

Kaṁsa: the wicked uncle of Śhrī Kṛiṣhṇa who was so hellbent on avoiding the prophecy of his impending death that he had ordered all newborns to be killed in his kingdom in an attempt to prevent the birth of Śhrī Kṛiṣhṇa.

kāṇḍa: section; chapter.

Karkidaka: name of the fourth month in July–August according to the Malayalam lunar calendar.

karma: action; mental, verbal, and physical activity; chain of effects produced by our actions.

karmic: having to do with the results of actions.

Karuka: *Cynodon dactylon*, a medicinal herb also known as Bermuda grass and Couch grass.

Kauravas: the one hundred children of King Dhṛitarāṣhṭra and Queen Gāndhārī, of whom the unrighteous Duryōdhana was the eldest. The Kauravas were the enemies of their cousins, the virtuous Pāṇḍavas, whom they fought against in the *Mahābhārata* War.

Kausalyā: one of the three wives of King Daśharatha, mother of Rāma.

Kerala: southernmost state of India bordering the Arabian Sea to the west, Tamil Nadu to the east, and Karnataka to the north.

Kiḷippaṭṭu: literally translating to 'parrot song.' A unique genre of Malayalam poetry.

Kṛiṣhṇa: from '*kṛiṣh,*' meaning 'to draw to oneself' or 'to remove sin;' principal incarnation of Lord Viṣhṇu. He was born into a royal family but raised by foster parents, and lived as a cowherd boy in Vṛindāvan, where he was loved and worshiped by his devoted companions, the *gōpīs* (milkmaids) and *gōpas* (cowherd boys). Kṛiṣhṇa later established the city of Dvāraka. He was a friend and advisor to his cousins, the Pāṇḍavas, especially Arjuna, whom he served as charioteer during the *Mahābhārata War*, and to whom he revealed his teachings as the *Bhagavad Gītā*.

Kumbhakarṇa: younger giant-brother of the demon king Rāvaṇa, known for his insatiable appetite, and sleeping for long periods of time. He is a formidable warrior, feared by many for his size and strength. He also had a sense of *dharma*, but chose to follow the path of unrighteousness out of loyalty to his elder brother Rāvaṇa, which ultimately led to his demise.

Kuśha: son of Rāma, twin-brother of Lava.

Lakṣhmaṇa: brother of Lord Rāma.

Laṅka: name of Rāvaṇa's kingdom popularly believed to have been situated in present day Sri Lanka.

Laṅkēśha: name of Rāvaṇa, lit. 'Lord of Laṅka.'

Lava: son of Rāma, twin-brother of Kuśha.

līlā: divine play.

Mahābhārata: ancient Indian epic that Sage Vyāsa composed, depicting the war between the righteous Pāṇḍavas and the unrighteous Kauravas.

mahāpuruṣha: a great enlightened personality with exceptional qualities and role as an exemplar for humanity.

maharṣhi: great *ṛiṣhi* or sage.

mahātmā: 'great soul;' term used to describe one who has attained spiritual realization.

Malayalam: language spoken in the Indian state of Kerala.

Malayali: one whose mother-tongue is Malayalam.

Mantharā: Kaikēyī's hunchbacked maid, who instigated the queen to demand that Daśharatha redeem his promise of giving her two boons: that Rāma be exiled from the kingdom to the forest for 14 years, and that the queen's own son, Bharata, be designated crown prince instead.

mantra: a sound, syllable, word or words of spiritual content. According to *Vēdic* commentators, *mantras* are revelations of *ṛiṣhis* arising from deep contemplation.

mantradṛiṣhṭā: lit. 'seer of *mantras*,' a sage to whom *mantras* were revealed.

Marāṭha: name of the empire that controlled a large portion of India in the 17th and 18th centuries.

Mārīcha: a *rākṣhasa* sent by Rāvaṇa who lured Rāma away from Sītā by taking the form of a golden deer.

mōkṣha: spiritual liberation, i.e. release from the cycle of births and deaths.

Nāgāstra: a powerful celestial weapon, or *astra*. *Nāgāstra*, meaning 'serpent arrow,' is also known as *nāgapaśha* ('serpent noose') and manifests as numerous venomous snakes that incapacitate or destroy the enemy when released. This weapon is often countered with the divine bird Garuḍa, who is the natural enemy of the serpents.

Nala: the *Vānara* architect and engineer who was tasked by Śhrī Rāma with the construction of the bridge to Laṇka.

Nārada: wandering sage ever engaged in singing the praises of Viṣhṇu. He composed the *Nārada Bhakti Sūtras*, aphorisms on devotion.

Narasiṁha: the fourth *avatār*, the man-lion incarnation of Lord Vişhṇu, who saved the devoted boy Prahlāda from his wicked father, the demon king Hiraṇyakaśhipu.

niyama: positive duties or observances (the 'dos'); the second 'limb' of the *aṣhṭāṅga yōga* (eight limbs) formulated by Sage Patañjali, and they include śhaucha (purity), *santōṣha* (contentment), *tapas* (austerity), *svādhyāya* (scriptural study) and īśhvara-praṇidhāna (contemplation of God); often mentioned in association with *yama*.

pādukā: traditional Indian footwear like sandals that may be used in worship symbolically representing the guru's auspicious feet.

Pāñchālī: another name for Draupadī, the wife of the five Pāṇḍava brothers.

Pāṇḍavas: five sons of King Pāṇḍu, and cousins of Kṛiṣhṇa, who are the main protagonists in the great *Mahābhārata* epic.

pāpa: sin; wrongdoing; demerit. Counterpart of *puṇya* (spiritual merit).

paramātman: supreme self, *brahman*.

Pārvatī: consort of Lord Śhiva.

Prahlāda: son of the demon king Hiraṇya-kaśhipu. Prahlāda had unswerving faith in Lord Viṣhṇu who appeared before him in the form of Narasiṁha — the man-lion *avatār* (incarnation).

prajā: citizens or people of a kingdom or nation.

pūjā: ritualistic or ceremonial worship.

pundit: scholar; knowledgeable person.

puṇya: spiritual merit. Counterpart of *pāpa*.

Purāṇas: compendium of stories, including the biographies and stories of gods, saints, kings and great people; allegories and chronicles of great historical events that aim to make the teachings of the *Vēdas* simple and available to all.

puruṣhārtha: the four goals of human life, namely *dharma* (righteous living), *artha* (pursuit of wealth), *kāma* (desire fulfillment), and *mōkṣha* (liberation from delusion).

rājā: king.

rājya: kingdom; reign.

rākṣhasa: demonic beings that derive pleasure from tormenting others.

rākṣhasī: female *rākṣhasa*; demoness.

Rāma: divine hero of the *Rāmāyaṇa*. An incarnation of Lord Viṣhṇu, he is considered the ideal man of *dharma* and virtue. 'Ram' means 'to revel;' one who revels in himself; the principle of joy within; one who gladdens the hearts of others.

Rāmachandra: another name of Lord Rāma.

Rāma Rājya: the ideal of selfless governance and righteous rule, inspired by Lord Rāma's reign in the Rāmāyaṇa. It prioritizes the welfare of the people, adherence to moral principles, and humble service to all citizens.

Rāmāyaṇa: 24,000-verse epic poem on the life and times of Lord Rāma.

Rāvaṇa: a powerful demon king. Although known to be a great *tapasvī* (performer of austerities) devoted to Lord Śhiva; an unparalleled scholar and musician well-versed in scriptures and the arts; and a competent ruler; Rāvaṇa, the King of Laṅka, could not desist from tormenting others due to his huge unrestrained ego. Lord Viṣhṇu incarnated as Lord Rāma to kill him, and thereby restore harmony to the world.

ṛiṣhi: seer to whom mantras are revealed in deep meditation.

sādhak (sādhaka): spiritual aspirant or seeker, one dedicated to attaining the spiritual goal, one who practices *sādhanā*.

sādhanā: regimen of disciplined and dedicated spiritual practice that leads to the supreme goal of self-realization.

samādhi: oneness with God; a state of deep, one-pointed concentration, in which all thoughts subside. The mind enters into a state of complete stillness in which only pure consciousness remains as one abides in the ātman or self.

saṁsāra: the cycle of birth and death; the world of plurality.

saṁskāra: *saṁskāras* are imprints or impressions left on the mind as a result of past experiences, actions, and thoughts (in this birth and also in prior births). These imprints shape an individual's character, tendencies, and reactions in future situations. *Saṁskāra* can also refer to the prevailing culture, or a particular deep-seated conditioning that shapes individuals, families, and society. The ritualistic ceremonies performed at significant stages of life, such as birth, marriage, and death, are also called *saṁskāras*.

Sanātana Dharma: 'Eternal Way of Life,' the original and traditional name of Hinduism.

saṅkalpa: divine resolve, usually used in association with *mahātmās*.

sannyāsin: a person who has renounced the material world, including family, career, and other attachments, to pursue a life devoted to spiritual practice and the pursuit of enlightenment or liberation (*mōkṣha*).

sārōpadēśha: composed of 'sāra (core)' + 'upadēśha (teaching)' literally meaning 'essential teaching.' *Sārōpadēśhas* are stories and texts that encapsulate the core teachings of Sanātana Dharma and offer moral guidance.

satgrantha: lit. 'book of truth;' sacred text or scripture dealing with spiritual truths and principles.

satguru: 'true master.' All *satgurus* are *mahātmās*, but not all *mahātmās* are *satgurus*. The *satguru* is one who, while still experiencing the bliss of the self, chooses to come down to the level of ordinary people in order to help them grow spiritually.

satsang: 'communion with the supreme truth.' Also, being in the company of *mahātmās*, studying the scriptures, and listening to the enlightening talks of a mahātmā; a meeting of people to listen to and/or discuss spiritual matters; a spiritual discourse.

sāttvic: pertaining to *sattva guṇa*; of pure quality; goodness.

ṣhaḍ darśhana: the six orthodox philosophical systems based on the *Vēdas*.

śhakti: personification of cosmic will and energy; strength; see *māyā*.

śhāstra: science; authoritative scriptural texts.

Śhatrughna: brother of Śhrī Rāma, twin brother of Lakṣhmaṇa and son of Sumitra.

Śhiva: the static aspect of *brahman* as the male principle. Worshiped as the first in the lineage of gurus, and as the formless substratum of the universe in relationship to the creative principle, Śhakti. He is the Lord of destruction in the trinity of Brahmā (Lord of creation), Viṣhṇu (Lord of preservation), and Śhiva. Usually depicted as a monk, with ash all over his body, snakes in his hair, wearing only a loincloth; he carries a begging bowl and a trident in his hands.

Śhivājī: Śhivājī Śhahajī Bhōnsalē, 1630 – 1680, King of the Marāṭha Empire. Also known as Chhatrapatī Śhivājī and as the disciple of Samarth Rāmdās.

śhraddhā: attentiveness; faith.

Śhūrpaṇakhā: a demoness and sister of Rāvaṇa. She took the form of a beautiful woman to entice first Rāma and then Lakṣhmaṇa. When rejected by both, she tried to attack Sītā, causing Lakṣhmaṇa to stop her by cutting off her nose.

siddha: lit. 'perfected,' a perfect or self-realized master

Sītā: Rāma's consort. In India, she is considered to be the ideal of womanhood.

smṛiti: 'what is remembered;' refers to sacred Hindu texts that are attributed to *ṛiṣhis*.

śhrī (Sri): a title of respect originally meaning 'divine,' 'holy,' or 'auspicious.'

Subhadrā: sister of Śhrī Kṛiṣhṇa, wife of Arjuna, and mother of the great warrior Abhimanyu.

Sumitrā: one of the three consort-queens of King Daśharatha of Āyōdhya, and mother of the twin half-brothers of Śhrī Rāma: Lakṣhmaṇa and Śhatrughna.

sundara kāṇḍa: 'Beautiful chapter' — the fifth 'book' of the *Rāmāyaṇa* and the only one to feature Hanumān as the main protagonist instead of Rāma.

svadharma: personal *dharma* or one's own duties.

tapas (tapasya): austerities, penance.

Trijaṭā: a demoness; the daughter of Vibhīṣhaṇa. She was given the duty of guarding Sītā when held captive in Laṅka.

tyāga: giving up, renunciation.

Upapurāṇas: considered supplementary to the 'major' *Purāṇas.*

Vālmīki: sage and author of the *Rāmāyaṇa.*

vanadēvatā: forest deity.

vānara: literally 'monkey' in Sanskrit. *Vānaras* are beings with ape-like features who, with their exceptional intelligence and strength, play a pivotal role in the *Rāmāyaṇa* as faithful servants of Lord Rāma.

vāsanā: latent tendency or subtle desire that manifests as thought, motive and action; subconscious impression gained from experience.

Vasiṣhṭha: revered ancient sage and guru to Lord Rāma and his brothers.

vasudhaiva kuṭumbakam: 'the world as one family' — a popular phrase from *Mahā Upaniṣhad*, 6.72.

Vaṭṭakudaṅgaḷ: *Centella asiatica*: Indian pennywort; a medicinal herb.

Vēdānta: 'end of *Vēda*.' The philosophy of the *Upaniṣhads*, the concluding part of the *Vēdas*, which holds the ultimate truth to be "one without a second." A *Vēdāntin* is a follower of *Vēdānta*.

Vēdas: the most ancient of all scriptures. Originating from God, the *Vēdas* were not composed by any human author but were 'revealed' in deep meditation to the ancient seers. These revelations came to be known as the *Vēdas*, of which there are four: *Ṛig*, *Yajur*, *Sāma*, and *Atharva*.

Vibhīṣhaṇa: younger demon-brother of Rāvaṇa who speaks out against the unrighteousness of his brother and subsequently surrenders himself to Lord Rāma.

vigraha: lit. 'shape; form; figure.' Physical representation or manifestation of a deity, such as a statue or an image used for worship.

Viṣhṇu: 'all-pervader,' Lord of sustenance in the trinity of Brahmā (Lord of creation), Viṣhṇu, and Śhiva (Lord of destruction).

Vyāsa: lit. 'compiler.' The name given to Sage Kṛiṣhṇa Dvaipāyana, who compiled the *Vēdas.* He is also the chronicler of the *Mahābhārata* and a character in it, and author of the eighteen *Purāṇas* and the *Brahma Sūtras.*

yajña: sacred acts of worship performed with the intent of offering something to the divine. Traditionally, a *yajña* consists of oblations offered into a fire according to scriptural injunctions accomanied by the chanting of sacred *mantras.* In a broader sense, a *yajña* may also comprise an act of selflessness performed with the intention of offering something for the welfare of others.

yama: restraints for proper conduct (the 'don'ts'); the first 'limb' of the *aṣhṭānga yōga* (eight limb path) formulated by Sage

Patañjali. They include *ahiṁsā* (non-violence), *satya* (truthfulness), *astēya* (non-stealing), *brahmacharya* (chastity) and *aparigraha* (non-covetousness); often mentioned in association with *niyama*.

yōga: 'to unite.' Union with the supreme being. A broad term, it also refers to the various methods of practices through which one can attain oneness with the divine. A path that leads to self-realization.

yōgī: a practitioner or an adept of *yōga*; *yoginī* is the female equivalent.

Pronunciation Guide

Vowels can be short or long:

a – as 'u' in 'but'	**ā** – as 'a' in 'far'
e – as 'a' in 'may'	**ē** – as 'a' in 'name'
i – as 'i' in 'pin'	**ī** – as 'ee' in 'meet'
o – as in 'oh'	**ō** – as 'o' in 'mole'
u – as 'u' in 'push'	**ū** – as 'oo' in 'hoot'
ṛi – as 'ri' in 'rim'	**ṛu** – as 'ru' in Spanish 'Peru'

ḥ – pronounce: **aḥ** like 'aha,' **iḥ** like 'ihi,' **uḥ** like 'uhu,' **ēḥ** like 'ēhē,' and **ōḥ** like 'ōhō.'

Some consonants are aspirated (e.g. kh); others are not (e.g. k):

k – as 'k' in 'kite'	**kh** – as 'ckh' in 'Eckhart'
g – as 'g' in 'give'	**gh** – as 'g-h' in 'dig-hard'
ch – as 'ch' in 'chat'	**chh** – as 'ch-h' in 'staunch-heart'
j – as 'j' in 'joy'	**jh** – as 'dgeh' in 'hedgehog'
p – as 'p' in 'pine'	**ph** – as 'ph' in 'up-hill'
b – as 'b' in 'bird'	**bh** – as 'bh' in 'rub-hard'

Pronounced with the tip of the tongue against the teeth:

t – as 't' in 'teach'	**th** – as 'th' in 'anthill'
d – as 'd' in 'door'	**dh** – as 'dh' in 'madhouse'

n – as ‘n’ in ‘night’

Retroflex sounds are produced by rolling the tongue back with the tip touching the roof of the mouth. The following examples can be used for practice:

ṭ – as ‘t’ in ‘tub’ **ṭh** – as ‘th’ in ‘lighthouse’
ḍ – as ‘d’ in ‘dove’ **ḍh** – as ‘dh’ in ‘red-hot’
ṇ – as ‘n’ in ‘naught’
ḷ – as ‘l’ in ‘revelry’ **ṣh** – as ‘sh’ in ‘shine’
zh – ‘rr’ in ‘hurray’ *(in Malayalam and Tamil)*

Other consonants:

y – as ‘y’ in ‘yes’ **r** – as ‘R’ in Italian ‘Roma’
l – as ‘l’ in ‘like’ **v** – as ‘v’ in ‘void’
śh – as ‘sh’ in ‘shepherd’ **s** – as ‘s’ in ‘sun’
m – as ‘m’ in ‘mother’ **h** – as ‘h’ in ‘hot’
ṅ – as ‘ng’ in ‘sing’ **ñ** – as ‘ny’ in ‘canyon’

Double consonants:

chch – as ‘tc’ in ‘hot chip’
jj – as ‘dj’ in ‘red jet’

"We have much to learn from each character of the Rāmāyaṇa. It is a storehouse of noble human values and spiritual principles. A person who reads or listens to the Rāmāyaṇa is purified. Devotion, knowledge, and detachment grow in such a person.

The Rāmāyaṇa should not remain only as the journey of Rāma. It should become our journey towards Rāma."

– Amma

www.ingramcontent.com/pod-product-compliance
Lightning Source LLC
LaVergne TN
LVHW051734080426
835511LV00018B/3050
* 9 7 8 1 6 8 0 3 7 9 1 2 9 *